Collins

CYCLING QUIZ BOOK

HarperCollins Publishers
Westerhill Road
Bishopbriggs
Glasgow
G64 2QT

First Edition 2013

Reprint 10 9 8 7 6 5 4 3 2 1 0

ISBN 978-0-00-752618-5

www.collinsdictionary.com

A catalogue record for this book is
available from the British Library

Typeset by Davidson Publishing
Solutions, Glasgow

Printed in Great Britain by Clays Ltd,
St Ives plc

Acknowledgements

AUTHOR
Chris Bradshaw

EDITOR
Ian Brookes

FOR THE PUBLISHER
Gerry Breslin
Lucy Cooper
Kerry Ferguson
Evelyn Sword

Introduction

They say that necessity is the mother of invention, and in the case of the bicycle that is certainly true. In the early nineteenth century there was an energy crisis: harvests were bad and the price of oats went up. Horses became expensive to feed so a bright spark in Germany called Karl Drais invented a human-powered two-wheeled vehicle, the precursor of the modern bicycle. Early bicycles didn't have pedals and the rider had to propel the vehicle with his feet, a system of locomotion expressed in the names for these early bikes: *velocipede* (French for 'swift feet') and *Laufmaschine* (German for 'running machine'). These inefficient vehicles never really caught on but when the chain-drive, pneumatic tyres, and gears were invented the bicycle's popularity rocketed.

There then followed a bicycling craze as millions took to two wheels for transport, fun, and then for racing. The first officially recorded bicycle race took place in Paris in 1868, velodromes were built in many cities so that racing could be done in front of a packed stadium, and cycling became so popular that it was included in the first modern Olympic Games in Athens in 1896. Since then, cycle racing has never looked back and the great champions are household names and even knights of the realm.

Collins Cycling Quiz Book tests your knowledge of cycling and how well you really know the sport. There are quizzes on all the classic races: the Giro d'Italia, the Vuelta a España and, of course, the Tour de France. There will be questions on British cycling legends, overseas cycling heroes, and you'll need to know your stuff on the Olympics too. All the cycling disciplines are covered – climbing, sprinting, track, and road racing – so there's something for everyone. It's the perfect way of whiling away the hours before you get out on your bike again.

The quizzes
The quizzes are grouped according to how tricky they are.
There's easy, then medium and then difficult quizzes.

Easy
If you're bike mad, then these questions are going to be a cycle
in the park. You'll be doing these 'no hands'. However, there are
a couple of tougher questions in the mix that might be labelled
as 'challenging' by some, so be warned. These have been
thrown in to add a few unexpected potholes on an otherwise
smooth journey.

Medium
If the easy questions are like coasting downhill, then this is
where the uphill part of the race begins. Be prepared to go down
a few gears and put on a sweat as the questions get tougher.

Difficult
These are the rounds that make legends. You'll need to have the
endurance, guts and cycling intelligence of Sir Bradley Wiggins
to come out on top of these. Anyone who gets all these questions
right deserves a yellow jersey, a gold medal, and a knighthood.

The answers
The answers to each quiz are printed at the end of the following
quiz. For example, the answers to Quiz 1-Pot Luck appear at the
bottom of Quiz 2-Tour de France part 1. The exception to this
rule is the last quiz in every level. The answers to these quizzes
appear at the end of the very first quiz in the level.

Running a quiz
Collins Cycling Quiz Book is only half-finished. (Wait! Don't
demand a refund yet, read on!) People don't go to the theatre
to sit and read a script. Likewise, the quizzes in this book need
someone to read them out. That's you.

If you're just quizzing your family during a car journey, or your mates of an afternoon, then there's probably no need to put in lots of preparation. If you're planning on using this book to run a more organized and formal quiz however, there are a few things you need to get right before you start:

❖ Rehearse: don't just pick this book up and read out the questions cold. Go through all the quizzes you're going to use by yourself beforehand. Note down all the questions (notes look better in a quiz environment than reading from a book) and answers. Although every effort has been made to ensure that all the answers in *Collins Cycling Quiz Book* are correct, despite our best endeavours, mistakes may still appear. If you see an answer you are not sure is right, or if you think there is more than one possible answer, then check.

❖ Paper and writing implements: do yourself a favour and prepare enough sheets of paper for everyone to write on. The aim of the game here is to stop the mad impulse certain people feel to 'help'. They will spend ten minutes running around looking for 'scrap' paper, probably ripping up your latest novel in the process. The same problem applies to pens. Ideally, have enough for everyone. Remember, though, that over half of them will be lost forever once you've given them out.

❖ Prizes: everyone likes a prize. No matter how small, it's best to have one on offer.

Good luck! We hope you enjoy *Collins Cycling Quiz Book*.

Contents

Easy Quizzes

Medium Quizzes

Difficult Quizzes

EASY QUIZZES

Quiz 1: Pot Luck

1. In which event did Sir Bradley Wiggins win gold at the 2012 London Olympics?

2. The national champion of which country wears a jersey that is a red, white, and blue tricolour?

3. What name is given to a rider who specializes in providing a wheel for a sprinter to follow in the final stages of a race?

4. Which three races are known collectively as the Grand Tours?

5. If all the teams that started the 2013 Tour de France were listed alphabetically, which would be first on the list?

6. Which diminutive climber could often be seen sporting a headscarf during races?

7. Which rider's Twitter profile reads, 'Fast sprinter, faster talker. Disclaimer: May cause offence'?

8. In which country did keirin racing originate?

9. Which common cycling term means 'little ball' in French?

10. Which flamboyant sprinter dressed up in a toga at the start of a stage of the 1999 Tour de France?

11. Up to 2013, how many times had the Tour de France started in the UK?

12. Alberto Contador joined which team in 2011?

13. Which was the only Australian team to take part in the 2013 Tour de France?

14. In 1992, who became the first winner of the Vélo d'Or awarded to the year's best cyclist?

15. Which two-time Tour de France winner died of cancer in August 2010, aged just 50?

16. Which British rider won Paris–Nice in 2012?

17. The Tour de Romandie is a stage race that takes place in which country?

18. Who was awarded the overall yellow jersey in the 2006 Tour de France after the disqualification of the original winner?

19. Lance Armstrong was stripped of how many Tour de France titles for doping offences?
    a) five
    b) six
    C) seven

20. What type of cake is also a famous Alpine climb?
    a) Bourbon
    b) Madeleine
    c) Stollen

Answers to Quiz 33: Pot Luck

1. Chris Froome	11. Cadel Evans
2. Sean Kelly	12. False
3. Stuart O'Grady	13. 15
4. A flat tyre	14. Gino Bartali
5. Bernard Hinault	15. Bianchi
6. Jacques Anquetil	16. False
7. Andy Schleck	17. Martin Earley
8. Two	18. After
9. Eddy Merckx	19. 37%
10. Greg LeMond	20. Bikes with gears

Quiz 2: Tour de France part 1

1. In which year did the 100th Tour de France take place?

2. What is the name of the 20-km long parade that precedes the riders on each stage of the Tour?

3. What name is given to the person in last place in the race?

4. What is the highest category of climb on the Tour?

5. Who is the only Irish rider to have won the Tour?

6. The Tour de France finishes each year on which famous thoroughfare?

7. At the Tour de France, each team starts with how many riders?

8. The 2013 Tour started on which island for the first time?

9. Which 40-year-old German was the oldest rider in the 2012 Tour?

10. What is the maximum age for a rider to be eligible for the White Jersey competition?

11. Who in 2011 became the first Australian to win the Tour?

12. Who won the best young rider competition in 2008, 2009, and 2010?

13. Which British rider wore yellow in 1994, 1997, and 1998?

14. The 2013 Tour featured how many team time trials?

15. Which Spaniard won the race five times between 1991 and 1995?

16. The Tour's team competition is decided by adding together the times of the top how many riders from each team?

17. Which Frenchman has won the King of the Mountains competition the most times?

18. Who was the first non-European to win the Tour?

19. In which year did the Tour de France take place for the first time?
    a) 1903
    b) 1913
    c) 1923

20. How many teams took part in 2013 Tour?
    a) 20
    b) 21
    c) 22

Answers to Quiz 1: Pot Luck

1. Road Time Trial
2. France
3. Lead-out man
4. Tour de France, Giro d'Italia, and Vuelta a España
5. AG2R-La Mondiale
6. Marco Pantani
7. Mark Cavendish
8. Japan
9. Peloton
10. Mario Cipollini
11. Once
12. Saxo-Tinkoff
13. Orica GreenEdge
14. Miguel Indurain
15. Laurent Fignon
16. Sir Bradley Wiggins
17. Switzerland
18. Oscar Pereiro
19. Seven
20. Madeleine

Quiz 3: Pot Luck

1. What colour jersey is worn by the leader of the Giro d'Italia?

2. The Schleck brothers are from which country?

3. Which divided city hosted the start of the 1987 Tour de France?

4. In which mountain range is the Col du Tourmalet?

5. Who was the first Canadian to win a Grand Tour?

6. Who was the first British rider to wear the leader's jersey at the Tour de France?

7. Laurent Fignon finished second in the 1989 Tour de France riding a bike made by which British manufacturer?

8. Which Irishman won a hat-trick of Tour de Romandie titles in 1983, 1984, and 1987?

9. Which Tour de France competition was originally called the Grand Prix Cinquentenaire?

10. Who was the first German to win the Tour de France?

11. Lance Armstrong was born in which American state?

12. Who are the two Swiss riders to have won the Vélo d'Or?

13. Which American rode his seventeenth Tour de France in 2012?

14. Who was the runner-up in the Tour de France points competition in both 2009 and 2010?

15. Sir Bradley Wiggins was born in which country?

16. Sir Bradley Wiggins, Chris Froome, and Robert Millar are three of the four British riders to have enjoyed a top ten Tour de France finish. Who is the fourth?

17. How many riders are awarded King of the Mountains points in the Tour de France on the highest category of climbs?

18. What type of race is known as the 'race of truth'?

19. Where was Mark Cavendish born?
    a) Isle of Man
    b) Isle of Sheppey
    c) Isle of Wight

20. In which year was the Olympic cycling team named Team of the Year at the BBC Sports Personality of the Year award ceremony?
    a) 2004
    b) 2008
    c) 2012

Answers to Quiz 2: Tour de France part 1

1. 2013	11. Cadel Evans
2. The caravan	12. Andy Schleck
3. Lanterne rouge	13. Chris Boardman
4. Hors catégorie	14. One
5. Stephen Roche	15. Miguel Indurain
6. Champs-Elysées	16. Three
7. Nine	17. Richard Virenque
8. Corsica	18. Greg LeMond
9. Jens Voigt	19. 1903
10. 25	20. 22

Quiz 4: Tour de France 2012

1. Who won the 2012 Tour de France?

2. Who finished second in the race?

3. Who was the third rider on the podium?

4. The first two stages of the race were held in which country?

5. Which French rider won the King of the Mountains competition?

6. Which four British riders won stages during the 2012 Tour?

7. Which Tour debutant won the Points competition?

8. Which Swiss rider wore the yellow jersey for the first week of the race?

9. Which team had the most stage wins in 2012?

10. How many riders started the 2012 Tour?

11. In addition to France, the 2012 Tour included a mountain stage in which country?

12. Including the prologue, the 2012 Tour featured how many stages?

13. Luis Leon Sanchez was one of two Spaniards to win a stage in 2012. Who was the other?

14. Which Russian, who won the 2009 Giro d'Italia, finished in 15th place?

15. Which three riders won three stages during the 2012 race?

16. Which Irishman finished in twelfth position?

17. Who was the highest-placed French finisher in the race?

18. Who were the somewhat surprising winners of the team competition?

19. How many stages did Sir Bradley Wiggins win in 2012?
    a) none
    b) one
    c) two

20. What was the race winner's overall margin of victory?
    a) 3m 21s
    b) 4m 21s
    c) 5m 21s

EASY

Answers to Quiz 3: Pot Luck

1. Pink
2. Luxembourg
3. Berlin
4. Pyrenees
5. Ryder Hesjedal
6. Tommy Simpson
7. Raleigh
8. Stephen Roche
9. Green jersey
10. Jan Ullrich
11. Texas
12. Tony Rominger and Fabian Cancellara
13. George Hincapie
14. Mark Cavendish
15. Belgium
16. Tommy Simpson
17. Ten
18. Time trial
19. Isle of Man
20. 2008

Quiz 5: Pot Luck

1. Who won the BBC Sports Personality of the Year Coach Award in 2012?

2. Who was the first Briton to hold the Tour de France green jersey for two consecutive days?

3. If all the teams that started the 2013 Tour de France were listed alphabetically, which would be last on the list?

4. Since its creation in 1992, who is the only Frenchman to have won the Vélo d'Or award?

5. 'L'arrivée' is the French for which part of a race?

6. Which Briton won the Tour de Romandie in 2012?

7. Who was stripped of victory in the 2006 Tour de France over a doping offence?

8. Excluding France, which country has hosted the opening stage of the Tour de France the most times?

9. Who is older – Frank Schleck or Andy Schleck?

10. Which veteran, who rode his 15th Tour de France in 2012, said, 'I am confident that when I get really old, the human lifespan will be extended'?

11. Who are the three English-born British riders to have worn the Tour de France yellow jersey?

12. Lance Armstrong came clean about his doping in an interview with which unlikely broadcaster?

13. Which flamboyant sprinter performed a wheelie while crossing the finish line at Gent–Wevelgem in 2013?

14. Sir Bradley Wiggins won gold at the 2004 Olympics in which event?

15. What is a wheel sucker?

16. Which mineral water company was an early sponsor of the UCI World Cup?

17. Who said, 'You need to make 100 split-second decisions in a sprint and they need to be right'?

18. The jersey worn by Team Europcar riders is primarily what colour?

19. What nationality is long-haired climber Daniel Moreno?
    a) Colombian
    b) Mexican
    c) Spanish

20. Riders from which of the following countries have won the most stages of the Tour de France?
    a) Australia
    b) Great Britain
    c) Ireland

Answers to Quiz 4: Tour de France 2012

1. Sir Bradley Wiggins
2. Chris Froome
3. Vincenzo Nibali
4. Belgium
5. Thomas Voeckler
6. Sir Bradley Wiggins, Mark Cavendish, David Millar, and Chris Froome
7. Peter Sagan
8. Fabian Cancellara
9. Team Sky
10. 198

11. Switzerland
12. 21
13. Alejandro Valverde
14. Denis Menchov
15. Mark Cavendish, Peter Sagan, and André Greipel
16. Nicolas Roche
17. Pierre Rolland
18. Radio Shack-Nissan
19. Two
20. 3m 21s

Quiz 6: Giro d'Italia

EASY

1. Who won the 2013 Giro d'Italia?

2. For which team was he riding?

3. In which month does the Giro usually start?

4. Who won the 2012 Giro d'Italia?

5. For which team was he riding?

6. Which Team Katusha rider from Spain finished second on the podium in 2012?

7. Which Italian, whose nickname is 'The Terrible', won the race in 2006 and 2010?

8. The 2012 Giro started in which Scandinavian country?

9. True or false – the Giro d'Italia has never started in England?

10. Traditionally (but not in 2013), the Giro has finished in which city?

11. What colour jersey is worn by the leader of the Mountains competition?

12. Who was promoted to race winner in 2011 after Alberto Contador had the title removed for doping?

13. Who is the only Briton to win the Best Climber prize at the Giro?

14. Who in 1995 became the third Swiss rider to win the race?

15. How many stages did the winner of the 2012 race win?

16. Who is the only French rider to have won a hat-trick of Giro titles?

17. Who is the only non-Italian to win the race five times?

18. The leader of the points competition in the Giro is awarded what colour jersey?

19. The Giro usually comprises how many stages?
    a) 21
    b) 22
    c) 23

20. In which year did the first Giro d'Italia take place?
    a) 1909
    b) 1919
    c) 1929

Answers to Quiz 5: Pot Luck

1. Sir Dave Brailsford
2. Mark Cavendish
3. Vacansoleil-DCM
4. Laurent Jalabert
5. The finish
6. Sir Bradley Wiggins
7. Floyd Landis
8. The Netherlands
9. Frank Schleck
10. Jens Voigt
11. Tommy Simpson, Sean Yates, and Chris Boardman
12. Oprah Winfrey
13. Peter Sagan
14. Individual pursuit
15. A rider who refuses to co-operate with pacemaking
16. Perrier
17. Mark Cavendish
18. Green
19. Spanish
20. Great Britain

Quiz 7: Pot Luck

EASY

1. Which cyclist rang the bell to mark the start of the opening ceremony inside the Olympic Stadium at the 2012 Games?

2. Which three races make up cycling's 'Triple Crown'?

3. True or false – Lance Armstrong never competed in the Giro d'Italia?

4. In a stage race, for what do the initials TTT stand?

5. In 2013, Mark Cavendish left Team Sky to join which team?

6. An occupational hazard of every cyclist, 'une crevaison' is the French word for what?

7. Which big name crashed on the climb of Luz Ardiden in 2003 after his handlebars became entangled with a spectator's handbag?

8. What were the two teams that took part in the 2013 Tour de France whose name starts with the letter B?

9. Who is the only German to have won the Vélo d'Or award?

10. What was the last Dutch city to host the start of the Tour de France?

11. True or false – there is a street in north London called Rue Bradley Wiggins?

12. In 2006, who became the first Briton to win the women's equivalent of the Tour de France?

13. The Gruyère Cycling Tour is an event that takes place in which country?

14. Who won the BBC Sports Personality of the Year Coach Award in 2008?

15. True or false – the colours on the rainbow jersey are the same as on the Olympic flag?

16. In 2004, who became the first British athlete for 40 years to win three medals at one Olympics?

17. For what do the initials UCI stand?

18. The classic children's bike the Chopper was made by which manufacturer?

19. What is Sir Bradley Wiggins' favourite band?
    a) Blur
    b) The Jam
    c) The Beatles

20. Who was the first Australian to win the Road World Championship?
    a) Phil Anderson
    b) Cadel Evans
    c) Robbie McEwen

Answers to Quiz 6: Giro d'Italia

1. Vincenzo Nibali	11. Blue
2. Astana	12. Michele Scarponi
3. May	13. Robert Millar
4. Ryder Hesjedal	14. Tony Rominger
5. Garmin-Barracuda	15. None
6. Joaquim Rodríguez	16. Bernard Hinault
7. Ivan Basso	17. Eddy Merckx
8. Denmark	18. Red
9. True	19. 21
10. Milan	20. 1909

Quiz 8: Tour de France part 2

1. Who said at his team's 2009 launch, 'Our aim is to win the Tour de France within five years'?

2. Which rider was dubbed 'Le Gentleman' by the French press during the 2012 race?

3. Who were the first pair of brothers to make the podium in the Tour de France in the same year?

4. Which Dane was kicked out of the 2007 Tour de France while wearing the yellow jersey?

5. Who celebrated a stage victory on the 2012 Tour de France by doing an impression of the Incredible Hulk when crossing the line?

6. True or false – the Tour once started in the former French colony of Algeria?

7. Which Spaniard claimed his only Tour de France victory in 1988?

8. True or false – the Tour de France used to feature days that included three split stages?

9. Who was the first World Champion to win the final stage of the Tour de France on the Champs-Elysées?

10. Was the 2013 Tour de France route largely staged in a clockwise or anticlockwise direction?

11. The Tour de France features how many rest days?

12. True or false – during a stage in the 1970s, the peloton rode so quickly that there was nobody at the finish to greet the first rider home?

13. Which team was expelled from the 1998 Tour after doping allegations?

14. Sir Bradley Wiggins enjoyed his first top ten Tour de France finish riding for which team?

15. In the Tour de France, what is 'le parcours'?

16. Kisso Kawamuro was the first rider from which country to take part in the Tour de France?

17. Which American electronics company took over the sponsorship of Team Blanco shortly before the start of the 2013 Tour de France?

18. Prior to Sir Bradley Wiggins, who was the last Tour de France winner who didn't defend his title a year later?

19. Which of the following sponsored a pro cycling team in the 1970s?
a) BHS b) C&A c) M&S

20. The third stage of the 2014 Tour is scheduled to finish in London. In which city will the stage start?
a) Birmingham b) Cambridge c) Oxford

EASY

Answers to Quiz 7: Pot Luck

1. Sir Bradley Wiggins
2. Tour de France, Giro d'Italia, and the Road World Cycling Championship
3. False
4. Team time trial
5. Omega Pharma-Quick Step
6. A puncture
7. Lance Armstrong
8. Belkin and BMC Racing Team
9. Jan Ullrich
10. Rotterdam
11. False
12. Nicole Cooke
13. Switzerland
14. Sir Dave Brailsford
15. True
16. Sir Bradley Wiggins
17. Union Cycliste Internationale
18. Raleigh
19. The Jam
20. Cadel Evans

Quiz 9: Pot Luck

1. Sprinter Peter Sagan is from which country?

2. Who was the first Olympic track gold medallist to win the Tour de France?

3. Downhill and 4-Cross are disciplines in which bike sport?

4. The start of the 2014 Tour de France will take place in which English county?

5. Who was the last Frenchman to win the Tour de France?

6. The Road World Championships usually follow which Grand Tour race?

7. In cycling, what is a 'sportive'?

8. Which British rider won the women's equivalent of the Tour de France in 2009?

9. The climb of Luz Ardiden is in which mountain range?

10. What were the two teams that took part in the 2013 Tour de France whose name starts with the letter C?

11. In 1998, who became the first Italian to win the Vélo d'Or award?

12. Miguel Poblet was the first rider from which country to wear the Tour de France yellow jersey?

13. Which race is colloquially known as the 'Race to the Sun'?

14. How many stage races had Ryder Hesjedal won before winning his maiden Giro d'Italia?

15. True or false – Eddy Merckx was awarded the honorary title of Baron by Belgium's King Albert II?

16. Which team managed to go through 12 consecutive Grand Tours (up to 2012) without a single rider dropping out?

17. What sort of race is run 'contre la montre'?

18. Which Briton finished second in the 1987 Giro d'Italia?

19. Excluding France, how many countries have hosted the start of the Tour de France?
a) seven
b) eight
c) nine

20. Who was the first British rider to win the 'Velo d'Or' award?
a) Mark Cavendish
b) Sir Chris Hoy
c) Sir Bradley Wiggins

Answers to Quiz 8: Tour de France part 2

1.	Sir Dave Brailsford	11. Two
2.	Sir Bradley Wiggins	12. True
3.	Frank and Andy Schleck	13. Festina
4.	Michael Rasmussen	14. Garmin-Slipstream
5.	Peter Sagan	15. The route
6.	False	16. Japan
7.	Pedro Delgado	17. Belkin
8.	True	18. Alberto Contador
9.	Mark Cavendish	19. C&A
10.	Clockwise	20. Cambridge

Quiz 10: Sprinters

EASY

1. Who won the Tour de France green jersey six consecutive times from 1996 until 2001?

2. 'The Terminator' is the nickname of which contemporary sprint star?

3. What nationality is John Degenkolb?

4. Who was the first Australian to win the green jersey at the Tour de France?

5. Which American sprinter was unlucky enough to crash four times during the first six stages of the 2012 Tour de France?

6. Who was the first British rider to win the points competition in all three Grand Tours?

7. Who is the only Italian rider to have completed the Grand Tour points hat trick?

8. Which German sprinter, riding for Argos-Shimano, won his second consecutive Scheldeprijs in 2013?

9. Which Italian sprinter won the Vélo d'Or award in 2002?

10. Who was the first rider from the former Soviet Union to win the green jersey at the Tour de France?

11. Who is the only Spaniard to have won the Tour de France green jersey?

12. Who performed a 'Forrest Gump running man'-style celebration after winning a stage of the 2012 Tour de France?

13. True or false – Robbie McEwen was a World Champion BMX rider before taking to the roads?

14. Who beat Mark Cavendish to the green jersey by just 9 points at the 2010 Tour de France?

15. Which Australian won his only Tour de France green jersey in 2003?

16. Which Belgian sprinter won an amazing 55 races during the 1976 season?

17. Who won four stages in a row during the 1999 Tour de France?

18. Which sprinter is nicknamed 'the Gorilla'?

19. What nationality is sprinter Alexander Kristoff?
    a) Danish b) Norwegian c) Swedish

20. How many green jersey points are awarded to the winner of a flat stage in the Tour de France?
    a) 20 b) 30 c) 45

Answers to Quiz 9: Pot Luck

1. Slovakia
2. Sir Bradley Wiggins
3. Mountain biking
4. Yorkshire
5. Bernard Hinault
6. Vuelta a España
7. An organized, mass-participation event, in which amateurs can take part
8. Emma Pooley
9. Pyrenees
10. Cannondale and Cofidis Solutions Credits
11. Marco Pantani
12. Spain
13. Paris–Nice
14. None
15. True
16. Liquigas
17. A time trial
18. Robert Millar
19. Nine
20. Sir Bradley Wiggins

Quiz 11: Pot Luck

1. What nationality is Tejay van Garderen?

2. What type of bicycle takes its name from two British coins?

3. Which Scot broke the one-hour speed record riding a bike called 'Old Faithful'?

4. Which French supermarket is the sponsor of the King of the Mountains jersey at the Tour de France?

5. What is a 'bidon'?

6. True or false – the front wheel of a bicycle travels further than the rear?

7. What is a 'triporteur'?

8. Which British woman won six Rainbow Jerseys between 1959 and 1968?

9. In 2013, Daryl Impey became the first rider from which country to wear the Tour de France yellow jersey?

10. Which fruit appeared in the name of a British trade team in the 1980s?

11. Who are the two British riders to have worn the Tour de France yellow jersey in their maiden appearance in the race?

12. What does it mean if a rider is suffering from the 'bonk'?

13. In which decade were dope tests first introduced to the Tour de France?

14. Who was the last rider to finish outside the top ten of the King of the Mountains competition to win the Tour de France?

15. What was the only team that took part in the 2013 Tour de France whose name starts with the letter E?

16. Who was the first Dutch rider to win the Vuelta a España?

17. Which controversial sprinter was thrown off the Vuelta a España in 2000 after punching Francisco Cerezo?

18. In 2004, a fan in Belgium made a triumphant arch for Tour de France riders to pass through that was made of what?
    a) Lego
    b) pasta
    c) toilet rolls

19. Where do races called 'criteriums' take place?
    a) city centres
    b) mountains
    c) velodromes

20. What sort rider is known in French as a 'grimpeur'?
    a) climber
    b) sprinter
    c) time trialist

EASY

Answers to Quiz 10: Sprinters

1. Erik Zabel
2. Peter Sagan
3. German
4. Robbie McEwen
5. Tyler Farrar
6. Mark Cavendish
7. Alessandro Petacchi
8. Marcel Kittel
9. Mario Cipollini
10. Djamolidine Abdoujaparov
11. Oscar Freire
12. Peter Sagan
13. True
14. Alessandro Petacchi
15. Baden Cooke
16. Freddy Maertens
17. Mario Cipollini
18. André Greipel
19. Norwegian
20. 45

Quiz 12: Team Sky

1. What colour jersey is worn by Team Sky?

2. Which noted coach is the team principal of Team Sky?

3. Who was the first Team Sky rider to wear the leader's jersey in a Grand Tour race?

4. Which Sky rider wore the polka dot jersey during the 2012 Tour de France?

5. What nationality is Edvald Boasson Hagen?

6. In which year did Team Sky make its Tour de France debut?

7. Which Swede was the team's best placed finisher in the team's Tour de France debut?

8. Which South American's 24th place finish was the best finish by a Team Sky rider on the 2011 Tour de France?

9. Who was the only British rider on Team Sky's 2013 Giro d'Italia team?

10. Chris Sutton was Sky's first stage-winner in a UCI Pro Tour race. In which 2010 event was he victorious?

11. Who won the mountainous stage 10 of the 2013 Giro d'Italia?

12. Which Team Sky rider won the British Road Race Championship in 2012?

13. Who was the first Team Sky rider to win a stage in the Tour de France?

14. Which Team Sky rider won Paris–Nice in 2013?

15. Who left his post as directeur sportif at Team Sky in October 2012?

16. Chris Froome beat Alberto Contador into second and Cadel Evans into third in the 2013 edition of which Asian race?

17. Who were the two Australians who were part of Team Sky at the 2012 Tour de France?

18. Who finished second in a classic 2011 stage to Arenberg, marking Team Sky's first podium appearance at the Tour de France?

19. What nationality is performance adviser Shane Sutton?
    a) Australian
    b) New Zealander
    c) South African

20. How many stages did Team Sky riders win during the 2012 Tour de France?
    a) four
    b) five
    c) six

Answers to Quiz 11: Pot Luck

1. American
2. Penny farthing
3. Graeme Obree
4. Carrefour
5. A plastic water-bottle
6. True
7. A three-wheeled bike
8. Beryl Burton
9. South Africa
10. Banana
11. Chris Boardman and David Millar
12. They have run out of energy
13. 1960s
14. Sir Bradley Wiggins
15. Euskaltel-Euskadi
16. Jan Janssen
17. Mario Cipollini
18. Toilet rolls
19. City centres
20. Climber

EASY

Quiz 13: Pot Luck

1. Prior to Mark Cavendish, who was the last Briton to win the World Road Race Championship?

2. 'Chute' is the French word for what unfortunate incident?

3. What nationality is Bernie Eisel?

4. Which Tour de France winner finished seventh in the men's cross-country mountain-bike race at the 2000 Olympics in Sydney?

5. 'Casque' is the French word for what?

6. Which was the only team that took part in the 2013 Tour de France whose name starts with the letter F?

7. In 2006, who became the third Italian to win the Vélo d'Or award?

8. Who won the Critérium du Dauphiné in 2012?

9. Who won 12 Tour de France stages between 1992 and 2004 but never completed the race?

10. In what way is a bearded German called Didi Senft a familiar figure on Tour de France stages?

11. Who finished runner-up to Ryan Giggs in the 2009 Welsh Sports Personality of the Year award?

12. What name is given to white-painted bikes that appear at fatal crash sites?

13. What nationality is former road race pro Julian Dean?

14. Often seen in the Tour de France, by what name is the 'voiture balai' known in English?

15. What is a 'dossard'?

16. The bike manufacturer Raleigh was originally based in which Midlands city?

EASY

17. In a stage race, for what do the initials GC stand?

18. What was Bradley Wiggins' number during the 2012 Tour de France?
   a) 101
   b) 121
   c) 131

19. In which year did the first American take part in the Tour de France?
   a) 1961
   b) 1971
   c) 1981

20. Who inadvertantly swore during a live TV interview after winning the opening stage of the 2013 Giro d'Italia?
   a) Mark Cavendish
   b) André Greipel
   c) Peter Sagan

Answers to Quiz 12: Team Sky

1. Black with a pale blue band
2. Sir Dave Brailsford
3. Sir Bradley Wiggins
4. Chris Froome
5. Norwegian
6. 2010
7. Thomas Lövkvist
8. Rigoberto Urán
9. Sir Bradley Wiggins
10. Tour Down Under
11. Rigoberto Urán
12. Ian Stannard
13. Edvald Boasson Hagen
14. Richie Porte
15. Sean Yates
16. Tour of Oman
17. Richie Porte and Michael Rogers
18. Geraint Thomas
19. Australian
20. Six

Quiz 14: Vuelta a España

1. Which Spanish rider won the 2012 Vuelta?

2. Since 2010, the leader of the race has worn what colour jersey?

3. In which month does the Vuelta a España usually take place?

4. What colour jersey is worn by the leader of the King of the Mountains competition?

5. Why was the race not held in the late 1930s?

6. Which Spaniard won the race in 2000, 2003, and 2004?

7. In 2012, what colour jersey was worn by the leader of the points competition?

8. Which British rider finished second in the Vuelta in 2011?

9. How many times did Miguel Indurain win the Vuelta?

10. Which Russian was victorious in 2005 and 2007?

11. True or false – the King of the Mountains jersey at one time featured brown coffee beans on a white jersey?

12. The Vuelta always finishes in which city?

13. Which city, famous for its bull run, hosted the opening stage of the 2012 Vuelta?

14. Who won the points competition for the first time in 2010?

15. Who enjoyed a hat-trick of Vuelta wins in 1992, 1993, and 1994?

16. Which British rider was the overall runner-up in both 1985 and 1986?

17. Who was the highest-placed British rider in the 2012 race?

18. Which Italian's first Grand Tour victory was in the 2010 Vuelta?

19. How many teams take part in the Vuelta?
    a) 20
    b) 21
    c) 22

20. The 2012 Vuelta comprised how many stages?
    a) 20
    b) 21
    b) 22

Answers to Quiz 13: Pot Luck

1. Tommy Simpson
2. A crash
3. Austrian
4. Cadel Evans
5. Helmet
6. FDJ (Francaise des Jeux)
7. Paolo Bettini
8. Sir Bradley Wiggins
9. Mario Cipollini
10. He dresses up as the devil
11. Geraint Thomas
12. Ghost bikes
13. New Zealander
14. Broom wagon
15. A racer's number
16. Nottingham
17. General classification
18. 101
19. 1981
20. Mark Cavendish

Quiz 15: Pot Luck

EASY

1. For what do the initials BMX stand?

2. The UK National Cycling Centre is in which city?

3. Which band had a number 11 hit in the UK charts in 1978 with 'Bicycle Race'?

4. Who was the first Norwegian to wear the yellow jersey at the Tour de France?

5. What colour jersey is awarded to the leader of the combined classification in the Vuelta a España?

6. Which stage race is sometimes known as the 'Race of the Two Seas'?

7. Which British rider won the 2012 Tour of Britain?

8. Which French word is used to describe a situation when the main group of riders fans out in a diagonal line to shelter from crosswinds?

9. The British Tour Series is televised on which TV channel?

10. In which month does the Critérium du Dauphiné traditionally take place?

11. In which country is Team Katusha based?

12. Which Australian won the Best Young Rider competition in the 2010 Giro d'Italia?

13. Which famous British cycling club, the oldest in the world, takes its name from a Charles Dickens novel?

14. In the Tour de France, what is a 'bonification'?

15. 'On the Road Bike: The Search for a Nation's Cycling Soul' is a 2013 book written by which broadcaster?

16. Which was the only team that took part in the 2013 Tour de France whose name starts with the letter G?

17. Who was the last reigning World Champion to win a stage of the Giro d'Italia?

18. What nationality is Team Sky rider Sergio Henao?

19. An injury to which part of the body caused Bradley Wiggins to miss the 2013 Tour de France?
    a) collar bone
    b) elbow
    c) knee

20. Vin Cox holds the record for the fastest circumnavigation of the globe on a bike. How long did it take him to complete the 29,330km?
    a) 153 days
    b) 163 days
    c) 173 days

Answers to Quiz 14: Vuelta a España

1. Alberto Contador
2. Red
3. September
4. White with blue polka dots
5. The Spanish Civil War was being fought
6. Roberto Heras
7. Green
8. Chris Froome
9. None
10. Denis Menchov
11. True
12. Madrid
13. Pamplona
14. Mark Cavendish
15. Tony Rominger
16. Robert Millar
17. Chris Froome
18. Vincenzo Nibali
19. 22
20. 21

Quiz 16: Classics

1. Which five races are known collectively as 'The Monuments'?

2. Who was forced to apologize after pinching the bottom of a 'podium girl' at the 2013 Tour of Flanders?

3. Which of the Schleck brothers won Liège–Bastogne–Liège in 2009?

4. Which race is known as 'The Hell of the North'?

5. Which Frenchman was the last rider to win a 'Monument' and the Tour de France in the same year?

6. In which month does Milan–San Remo take place?

7. Who won Paris–Roubaix for the third time in 2013?

8. Which Garmin rider in 2013 became the second Irish winner of Liège–Bastogne–Liège?

9. Who edged out Filippo Pozzato and Alessandro Ballan to win the 2012 Tour of Flanders?

10. The Tour of Flanders starts in which scenic Belgian town?

11. Which classic is known as 'La Doyenne'?

12. Which British rider won Milan–San Remo in 2009?

13. Who holds the record for the most wins in the five one-day 'Monuments'?

14. Which Belgian won Paris–Roubaix in 2005, 2008, 2009, and 2012?

15. What is the only one of 'The Monuments' that takes place in autumn?

16. Who completed a clean sweep of Amstel Gold Race, Flèche Wallonne, and Liège–Bastogne–Liège wins in 2011?

17. Who is the only Irishman to win Paris–Roubaix?

18. Which sprinter won Milan–San Remo in 1997, 1998, 2000, and 2001?

19. How many times did Lance Armstrong win Paris–Roubaix?
a) never
b) once
c) twice

20. Approximately how much of the 260km Paris–Roubaix course is raced over cobbles?
a) 10km
b) 30km
c) 50km

EASY

Answers to Quiz 15: Pot Luck

1. Bicycle motocross
2. Manchester
3. Queen
4. Thor Hushovd
5. White
6. Tirreno–Adriatico
7. Jonathan Tiernan-Locke
8. Echelon
9. ITV4
10. June
11. Russia
12. Richie Porte
13. Pickwick CC (from the Pickwick Papers)
14. A time bonus
15. Ned Boulting
16. Garmin-Sharp
17. Mark Cavendish
18. Colombian
19. Knee
20. 163 days

Quiz 17: Pot Luck

EASY

1. What is the name of the motorcycle used in keirin and six-day races?

2. Each team in the Men's World Championship Road Race is made up of how many riders?

3. What French word, meaning 'servant', is used to describe a rider who helps the team leader?

4. Which British rider broke the one-hour world record at Manchester on 27 October 2000?

5. Which country is the largest bicycle manufacturer in the world?

6. Only one team that took part in the 2013 Tour de France had a name that started with the letter K. Which one?

7. Which city in the Basque Country hosted the start of the 1992 Tour de France?

8. Which Irishman took part in the Tour de France three times in the 1980s, enjoying a best finish of 131st in 1986?

9. Results in the British Tour Series are determined by adding together the finishing position of how many riders from each team?

10. Which Swede was runner-up in the 2012 Tour de France King of the Mountains competition?

11. Whom was Mark Cavendish describing when he said, 'He is super, super good. He's making us all look like juniors'?

12. Which Formula One World Champion is the owner of the UK Youth cycling team?

13. True or false – the Giro d'Italia has previously started in the Vatican City?

14. Which Australian pro has the same name as a member of 1980s boy band Bros?

15. How long is a single lap of an Olympic velodrome?

16. A stage race called the Arctic Race takes place in which country?

17. Which pre-Tour de France stage race was won by Sir Bradley Wiggins in both 2011 and 2012?

18. Which TV commentator started the Tour de France seven times between 1978 and 1985, completing five of them?

19. What nationality is Cofidis leader Rein Taaramäe?
    a) Estonian
    b) Latvian
    c) Lithuanian

20. What does Cipollini mean in English?
    a) apple
    b) garlic
    c) onion

Answers to Quiz 16: Classics

1. Milan–San Remo, Tour of Flanders, Liège–Bastogne–Liège, Giro di Lombardia, Paris–Roubaix
2. Peter Sagan
3. Andy Schleck
4. Paris–Roubaix
5. Bernard Hinault
6. March
7. Fabian Cancellara
8. Dan Martin
9. Tom Boonen
10. Bruges
11. Liège–Bastogne–Liège
12. Mark Cavendish
13. Eddy Merckx
14. Tom Boonen
15. Giro di Lombardia
16. Philippe Gilbert
17. Sean Kelly
18. Erik Zabel
19. Never
20. 50km

EASY

Quiz 18: The 2012 Olympics

1. Who was the first British cyclist to win a gold medal at London 2012?

2. Which country topped the medal table in cycling events at London 2012?

3. Who won the Men's Road Race at London 2012?

4. Which cyclist carried the British flag at the Opening Ceremony?

5. Who won gold in the Men's Sprint at London 2012?

6. Who were the five members of Britain's ill-fated Men's Road Race Team?

7. Who was the highest placed British finisher in the Men's Road Race?

8. The Individual Road Time Trials took place at which famous royal palace?

9. Laura Trott won gold in which individual event?

10. Which Briton won bronze in the Men's Individual Road Time Trial?

11. The Road Races at London 2012 started and finished on which famous thoroughfare?

12. Which Australian woman won the Women's Individual Sprint gold?

13. Which Dane won the Men's Omnium in London?

14. Which British trio won gold in the Women's Team Pursuit at London 2012?

15. Which country did Britain beat in the Women's Team Pursuit final?

16. British gold medal winner Philip Hindes was born in which country?

17. Name the quartet of British riders who won gold in the final of the Men's Team Pursuit at London 2012.

18. Which team did they beat in that final?

19. How many medals did the British track team win at London 2012?
    a) seven
    b) eight
    c) nine

20. How many of those medals were gold?
    a) seven
    b) eight
    c) nine

Answers to Quiz 17: Pot Luck

1. Derny
2. Nine
3. Domestique
4. Chris Boardman
5. China
6. Katusha
7. San Sebastián
8. Paul Kimmage
9. Three
10. Fredrik Kessiakoff
11. Peter Sagan
12. Nigel Mansell
13. True
14. Matt Goss
15. 250m
16. Norway
17. Critérium du Dauphiné
18. Paul Sherwen
19. Estonian
20. Onion

Quiz 19: Pot Luck

1. By what name is the race 'Ronde van Vlaanderen' known in English?

2. Which country hosted the 2013 World Track Championships?

3. Which cyclist appeared on the TV show 'Strictly Come Dancing' in 2012?

4. The National Indoor BMX Arena is in which English city?

5. Which German rider won the 2013 Milan–San Remo?

6. How many teams featured in the 2013 Tour de France?

7. Which Norwegian rider won the Tour of Britain in 2009?

8. In the Tour de France, the 'flame rouge' indicates there is how long left to go?

9. Which track event is also known as the kilo?

10. Who was the first Belgian to win the Giro d'Italia?

11. What colour jersey was worn by members of the leading team in the 2013 British Tour Series?

12. Which breakfast-cereal manufacturer sponsored the Tour of Britain between 1987 and 1994?

13. Which green jersey winning sprinter won the Junior World Championship in mountain biking in 2008?

14. In 2012, which team signed a rider who was not from the Basque Country for the first time?

15. Prior to 2010, by what name was the Critérium du Dauphiné known?

16. Which cyclist was awarded the freedom of the City of Edinburgh in 2012?

17. What were the two teams that started the 2013 Tour de France whose names start with the letter L?

18. Sir Bradley Wiggins' first podium finish in a Grand Tour event came in which race?

19. Which of the following is the name of a professional cyclist?
    a) Roberto Ferrari
    b) Roberto Fiat
    c) Roberto Mercedes

20. Which of these countries has not hosted the opening stage of the Giro d'Italia?
    a) Belgium
    b) England
    c) Greece

Answers to Quiz 18: The 2012 Olympics

1. Sir Bradley Wiggins
2. Great Britain
3. Alexandre Vinokurov
4. Sir Chris Hoy
5. Jason Kenny
6. Mark Cavendish, Bradley Wiggins, David Millar, Chris Froome, and Ian Stannard
7. Mark Cavendish (in 29th)
8. Hampton Court
9. Omnium
10. Chris Froome
11. The Mall
12. Anna Meares
13. Lasse Norman Hansen
14. Danielle King, Joanna Rowsell, and Laura Trott
15. USA
16. Germany
17. Burke, Clancy, Kennaugh, Thomas
18. Australia
19. Nine
20. Seven

Quiz 20: Olympic Cycling

1. Over what distance is the Men's Team Pursuit contested?

2. Which cyclist is the most successful Scottish Olympian of all time?

3. What are the four disciplines of Olympic cycling?

4. How many laps of the track is an Olympic Men's Sprint?

5. How many different disciplines make up an omnium?

6. True or false – tandem racing used to be an Olympic event?

7. In 2008, who became the first British woman to win a medal in two different sports?

8. In addition to cycling gold, the sportswoman in the question above earned a silver in which sport?

9. Over what distance is the Olympic Women's Team Pursuit contested?

10. How many riders take part in an Olympic keirin race?

11. Which Spaniard won the Men's Road Race in 2008?

12. What is the first element of an Olympic omnium?

13. What name is given to the round in which losers of previous heats race against each other in a bid to get back into the competition?

14. Which Briton won the Women's Road Race in 2008?

15. What is the final event of an Olympic Men's Omnium?

16. Who are the three riders to have won the Tour de France and an Olympic gold medal?

17. Who won Britain's only cycling medal at the 1992 games in Barcelona?

18. In which event did the successful rider claim gold?

19. An Olympic keirin race consists of how many laps of the track?
    a) seven
    b) eight
    c) nine

20. How many gold medals did the British track team win at the 2008 Beijing games?
    a) three
    b) five
    c) seven

EASY

Answers to Quiz 19: Pot Luck

1. Tour of Flanders
2. Belarus
3. Victoria Pendleton
4. Manchester
5. Gerald Ciolek
6. 22
7. Edvald Boasson Hagen
8. 1km
9. 1000m time trial
10. Eddy Merckx
11. Red
12. Kellogg's
13. Peter Sagan
14. Euskaltel-Euskadi
15. Critérium du Dauphiné Libéré
16. Sir Chris Hoy
17. Lampre-Merida and Lotto-Belisol
18. Vuelta a España
19. Roberto Ferrari
20. England

Quiz 21: Pot Luck

1. 'La Primavera' is the nickname of which Classic?

2. The Olympic Men's Team Pursuit is a race over how many laps of the track?

3. Wendy Houvenaghel was born and brought up in which country of the UK?

4. In an Olympic Women's Omnium, the time trial takes place over what distance?

5. 'The Assassin' is the nickname of which East European Grand Tour winner?

6. What was the only 2013 Tour de France team whose name starts with the letter M?

7. Who caused controversy during the 2012 Tour de France by autographing a fan's breasts before the start of a stage?

8. Which politician said, 'I hope that cycling in London will become almost Chinese in its ubiquity'?

9. Prior to joining Team Sky, Sir Bradley Wiggins rode for which team?

10. Who claimed his second Tour of Flanders victory in 2013?

11. Who broke his pelvis after crashing during a perilous time trial during the 2012 Critérium du Dauphiné?

12. In Tour de France team time trials, the team's finishing time is recorded when the rider in which place crosses the line?

13. What is a 'poisson pilot'?

14. Which cycling legend was born in Meensel-Kiezegem, Belgium?

15. 'Believe in Better' is the motto of the sponsor of which team?

16. How many teams featured in the 2013 Giro d'Italia?

17. True or false – Bradley Wiggins, Chris Froome, and Mark Cavendish all abandoned the 2012 World Championship Road Race?

18. Which race translates into English as Tour of the Future?

19. Olympic sprint races are contested in a best of how many format?
    a) one
    b) three
    c) five

20. How many riders have won the Giro d'Italia, Tour de France, and Vuelta a España in the same year?
    a) none
    b) one
    c) two

EASY

Answers to Quiz 20: Olympic Cycling

1. 4000m
2. Sir Chris Hoy
3. Track, road, BMX, and mountain biking
4. Three
5. Six
6. True
7. Rebecca Romero
8. Rowing
9. 3000m
10. Six
11. Samuel Sanchez
12. Flying lap
13. Repechage
14. Nicole Cooke
15. 1km time trial
16. Bradley Wiggins, Miguel Indurain, and Jan Ullrich
17. Chris Boardman
18. Individual pursuit
19. Eight
20. Seven

Quiz 22: Road World Championships

EASY

1. The Road World Championships are usually held in which month?

2. Which Briton won silver in the Men's Time Trial at the 2011 World Championships?

3. Do individual World Championship races feature trade teams or national teams?

4. Which Belgian won the 2012 World Championship road race?

5. Which European country will host the 2014 Road World Championships?

6. Which British rider won the silver medal in the 2010 World Championship time trial?

7. Who was the last winner of the World Road Race Championship whose surname starts with a vowel?

8. Which Australian won a hat-trick of Road World Championship time trials in 2003, 2004, and 2005?

9. Who was the first Scandinavian to win the Men's Road Race World Championship?

10. Which Briton won the first World Championship road time trial?

11. In which year of the 1990s did that first World Championship individual time trial take place?

12. Who is the only American to win the World Championship road race more than once?

13. Who was the first British rider to win the Women's Road World Championship?

14. True or false – the Road World Championships have never been hosted in Ireland?

15. With four wins up to 2012, who has won the most Road World Championship time trial titles?

16. In 1997, who became the first (and so far only) French rider to win the Road World Championship time trial?

17. Who was the last rider whose surname ends in a vowel to win the World Road Race Championship?

18. Which Team Sky rider won silver in the 2011 men's road race?

19. Which country will host the 2015 Road World Championships?
    a) UAE b) UK c) USA

20. How often do the World Championships take place?
    a) every year b) every two years c) every four years

Answers to Quiz 21: Pot Luck

1. Milan–San Remo
2. 16
3. Northern Ireland
4. 500m
5. Denis Menchov
6. Movistar
7. Peter Sagan
8. Boris Johnson
9. Garmin-Slipstream
10. Fabian Cancellara
11. Andy Schleck
12. Fifth
13. A French phrase for a lead-out man
14. Eddy Merckx
15. Team Sky
16. 23
17. True
18. Tour de l'Avenir
19. Three
20. None

Quiz 23: Pot Luck

1. What are the three Ardennes Classics?

2. In which month does the Tour of Britain usually take place?

3. 'La Corsa Rosa' is the nickname of which race?

4. The winner of which single-day classic receives a mounted cobble known as a sett?

5. Two 2013 Tour de France teams have names that start with the letter O. Which two?

6. In which year did the first Olympic omnium event take place?

7. True or false – Chris Boardman is the nephew of Scouse comedian Stan Boardman?

8. What is the name of a cotton bag containing food and drink that is handed out to riders?

9. The bane of many an urban cycle ride, what are known in France as 'ralentisseurs'?

10. Who is the only rider to have won all five 'Monuments', the World Championship Road Race, and all three Grand Tours?

11. Who won the Tour of Norway for the second successive year in 2013?

12. The name of which mythological character was also the name of a British trade team that made its Tour de France debut in 1955?

13. In 1996, who became the first Belgian to win the Vélo d'Or award?

14. For the first time in 24 years, a stage of the Giro d'Italia had to be cancelled in 2013. What was the reason?

15. 17 of the 22 teams selected for the 2013 Tour de France wore kit that contained which colour?

16. Fines at the Tour de France are levied in which currency?

17. Do national championships take place just before or just after the Tour de France?

18. Which Briton wore the white jersey during the opening week of the 2011 Tour de France?

19. What nationality is Lotto-Belisol rider Greg Henderson?
   a) Australia
   b) Canadian
   c) New Zealander

20. Which of these countries has not hosted the opening stage of the Tour de France?
   a) Denmark
   b) Monaco
   c) Switzerland

Answers to Quiz 22: Road World Championships

1.	September	11.	1994
2.	Sir Bradley Wiggins	12.	Greg LeMond
3.	National teams	13.	Beryl Burton
4.	Philippe Gilbert	14.	True
5.	Spain	15.	Fabian Cancellara
6.	David Millar	16.	Laurent Jalabert
7.	Cadel Evans	17.	Paolo Bettini
8.	Michael Rogers	18.	Edvald Boasson Hagen
9.	Thor Hushovd	19.	USA
10.	Chris Boardman	20.	Every year

Quiz 24: Climbers

1. Who was the last rider to win the Tour de France King of the Mountains competition whose first name and surname start with the same letter?

2. Who won the Tour de France summit finishes at Morzine-Avoriaz and the Tourmalet in 2010 and at the Galibier in 2011?

3. Which Colombian climber was known as 'Lucho'?

4. Riders from which country have won the King of the Mountains jersey at the Tour de France the most times?

5. Which noted climber was once described as looking like 'a Dickensian chimney-sweep'?

6. Which Tour de France King of the Mountains winner said, 'I've never been a winged climber. I regard this as a symbol of my combativeness'?

7. 'The Angel of the Mountains' was the nickname of which Luxembourger Tour de France winner?

8. Which multiple Tour de France King of the Mountains winner was born in Casablanca?

9. 'Purito' (little cigar) is the nickname of which Spanish climber?

10. 'The Road Uphill' is a documentary about which cycling brothers?

11. Which Italian won stages at Alpe d'Huez in 1995 and 1997?

12. 'The Eagle of Toledo' was a nickname of which legendary Spanish climber?

13. Which Tour de France King of the Mountains winner broke his collar bone during the 2013 Amstel Gold race?

14. Who is the only Swiss rider to have won the Tour de France King of the Mountains competition?

EASY

15. Which Frenchman, riding for Team Europcar, won his first Tour de France King of the Mountains title in the 2010 race?

16. Which Belgian Tour de France winner, who enjoyed great success in the mountains, started and finished the race 15 times between 1969 and 1985?

17. Which Spanish climber, and future winner, looked set to win the 1971 Tour de France until a crash involving Eddy Merckx and two other riders forced him to abandon?

18. Which Belgian climber finished fourth overall in the Tour de France in both 2010 and 2012?

19. What nationality is Nairo Quintana?
    a) Colombian b) Spanish c) Venezuelan

20. What was the animal-related nickname of climber Jacques Marinelli?
    a) the budgie b) the condor c) the vulture

Answers to Quiz 23: Pot Luck

1. Amstel Gold Race, Flèche Wallonne, and Liège-Bastogne-Liège
2. September
3. Giro d'Italia
4. Paris–Roubaix
5. Omega Pharma-Quick Step and Orica GreenEdge
6. 2012
7. False
8. Musette
9. Speed bumps
10. Eddy Merckx
11. Edvald Boasson Hagen
12. Hercules
13. Johan Museeuw
14. Heavy snow
15. Blue
16. Swiss francs
17. Just before
18. Geraint Thomas
19. New Zealander
20. Denmark

Quiz 25: Pot Luck

1. In which month does the Tour of Flanders take place?

2. The Tirreno–Adriatico takes place in which country?

3. The 'maillot à pois rouges' is the French name for which jersey?

4. The bicycle manufacturer Giant is based in which country?

5. True or false – Cadel Evans didn't win a major mountain stage in his first eight Tour de France appearances?

6. Which American author and humourist wrote, 'Learn to ride a bicycle. You will not regret it if you live'?

7. Which team had four finishers in the top ten in the 2012 Critérium du Dauphiné?

8. The Col d'Aspin is in which mountain range?

9. Which 36-year-old in 2013 became the oldest rider to make the podium of a Grand Tour event since 1928?

10. After which rider is a station on the Brussels metro named?

11. The 2013 Tour de France featured one team whose name starts with the letter R. Which one?

12. Which cyclist was voted Spain's athlete of the 20th century?

13. What is the only Dutch one-day classic that is a UCI World Tour event?

14. Which Scottish-born inventor created the world's first working air-filled rubber tyre?

15. Which rider-turned-journalist won the William Hill Sports Book of the Year award in 1990?

16. True or false – the winner of the first Tour de France was awarded a green armband rather than the yellow jersey?

17. Which 2012 Olympic gold medallist has the same surname as a member of England's Ashes winning 2010/11 cricket team?

18. Who won a hat-trick of Vélo d'Or awards in 2007, 2008, and 2009?

19. Which race is also known as 'La Classicissima'?
    a) Giro di Lombardia
    b) Milan–San Remo
    c) Vuelta a España

20. How long is the bike-ride element of an Olympic triathlon?
    a) 40km
    b) 43km
    c) 46km

Answers to Quiz 24: Climbers

1. Samuel Sanchez	11. Marco Pantani
2. Andy Schleck	12. Federico Bahamontes
3. Luis Herrera	13. Thomas Voeckler
4. France	14. Tony Rominger
5. Robert Millar	15. Anthony Charteau
6. Laurent Jalabert	16. Lucien Van Impe
7. Charly Gaul	17. Luis Ocaña
8. Richard Virenque	18. Jurgen Van Den Broeck
9. Joaquim Rodriguez	19. Colombian
10. Andy and Frank Schleck	20. The Budgie

Quiz 26: Anagrams

Rearrange the letters to make the name of a Tour de France winner.

1. Badge grins wily

2. Lend em grog

3. Map carnation

4. Lab rigatoni

5. Chill nu jar

6. Khans cycled

7. Stores rascal

8. I mainlined guru

9. Ciao soft pup

10. Jet elk poem zoo

11. Fungal intoner

12. Hornets cheep

13. Liven up cinema

14. Bible out soon

15. Doctoral baronet

EASY

16. A jib errs in

17. I turn handlebar

18. Save candle

19. Degraded polo

20. Casual ion

Answers to Quiz 25: Pot Luck

1. April
2. Italy
3. Polka-dot jersey
4. Taiwan
5. True
6. Mark Twain
7. Team Sky
8. Pyrenees
9. Cadel Evans
10. Eddy Merckx
11. Radioshack
12. Miguel Indurain
13. Amstel Gold
14. John Boyd Dunlop
15. Paul Kimmage
16. True
17. Laura Trott
18. Alberto Contador
19. Milan–San Remo
20. 43km

Quiz 27: Pot Luck

1. In which month does Paris–Roubaix take place?

2. What is the name of the event that allows amateur cyclists to race over the same route as a Tour de France stage?

3. Who won Paris–Nice seven years in a row between 1982 and 1988?

4. Which famous author said, 'Whenever I see an adult on a bicycle, I do not despair for the future of the human race'?

5. What Italian word, meaning 'little group', is used to describe the last bunch of riders on a mountain stage?

6. What is the French equivalent for that term?

7. 'Poupou' was the nickname of which Tour de France nearly man?

8. CTC are the initials of which organization?

9. Which material, beloved of cyclists, was invented by Joseph Shivers of DuPont in 1958?

10. Greg LeMond won his first Tour de France riding for which French team?

11. Who claimed his first professional victory partnering Patrick Sercu in the Six Days of Ghent in 1966?

12. Which Irish cyclist was born in Dundrum, Dublin on 28 November 1959?

13. Is the Tour of Switzerland held before or after the Tour de France?

14. True or false – Chris Boardman has won the BBC Sports Personality of the Year award?

15. Which Belgian won the 2011 Vélo d'Or award?

16. Which four Italian races are part of the UCI World Tour?

17. In the Tour de France what is a 'zone de ravitaillement'?

18. Who rides a bike nicknamed 'The Tourmanator'?

19. What has happened to a rider who has 'shelled'?
    a) they've crashed
    b) they can't keep up with the bunch
    c) they've collected food for the rest of the team

20. Which French word describes a rider who is especially strong on long, rolling flat stages?
    a) grimpeur
    b) rouleur
    c) soigneur

EASY

Answers to Quiz 26: Anagrams

1. Bradley Wiggins
2. Greg LeMond
3. Marco Pantani
4. Gino Bartali
5. Jan Ullrich
6. Andy Schleck
7. Carlos Sastre
8. Miguel Indurain
9. Fausto Coppi
10. Joop Zoetemelk
11. Laurent Fignon
12. Stephen Roche
13. Lucien Van Impe
14. Louison Bobet
15. Alberto Contador
16. Bjarne Riis
17. Bernard Hinault
18. Cadel Evans
19. Pedro Delgado
20. Luis Ocaña

Quiz 28: Team Sponsors

What is the industry of the primary sponsor of the following teams? eg Team Sky – Broadcasting

1. Cannondale

2. Team Europcar

3. Euskaltel

4. Cofidis

5. FDJ

6. Movistar

7. BMC Racing

8. Orica-GreenEdge

9. Sojasun

10. Radioshack

11. Team Argos

12. Team Saxo-Tinkoff

13. Lampre

14. Garmin

15. Vacansoleil-DCM

16. Vini Fantini

17. Rapha Condor

18. Kas

19. Z

20. Linda McCartney

Answers to Quiz 27: Pot Luck

1. April
2. L'Étape du Tour
3. Sean Kelly
4. HG Wells
5. Gruppetto
6. Autobus
7. Raymond Poulidor
8. Cyclists' Touring Club
9. Lycra
10. La Vie Claire
11. Eddy Merckx
12. Stephen Roche
13. Before
14. False
15. Philippe Gilbert
16. Tirreno–Adriatico, Milan–San Remo, Giro d'Italia, and Giro di Lombardia
17. Areas where riders can be given food
18. Peter Sagan
19. They can't keep up with the bunch
20. Rouleur

Quiz 29: Pot Luck

1. In which month does the Giro di Lombardia take place?

2. Team Astana is named after the capital city of which country?

3. In which year did Greg LeMond win his final Tour de France?

4. In France it's known as a 'sprint massif', but what is it known as in English?

5. Who was named 'The Greatest Ever Belgian' by Humo magazine in 2004?

6. Which two-time British Road Race Champion has the same name as a Conservative MP and cabinet minister?

7. Who became the second Irishman to win the Volta a Catalunya in 2013?

8. Which other Irish rider won the Volta a Catalunya in both 1984 and 1986?

9. 'Terse pagan' is an anagram of which contemporary rider?

10. Which car manufacturer sponsored the Tour of Ireland between 1985 and 1992?

11. Which Portuguese rider won the Tour of Switzerland in 2012?

12. True or false – points allocated for the best climber classification were doubled for summit finishes at the 2013 Tour de France?

13. Which American pioneered the use of tri-bars on time-trial bikes?

14. Which two Italian greats was national manager Alfredo Binda describing when he said, 'It was like being asked to put a cat and a dog in the same sack'?

15. Who was Team Sky's captain on the road during the 2012 Tour de France?

16. Which American exchanged blows with Jeroen Blijlevens following a controversial stage of the 2000 Tour de France?

17. Which British rider's only major road win as an amateur was the 1993 Tour of Lancashire?

18. Which race, founded in 1961, is considered a Tour de France for young riders?

19. Approximately how many calories does the average rider burn off during a stage of a Grand Tour race?
    a) 3,500
    b) 5,500
    c) 7,500

20. Which English county does Sir Bradley Wiggins now call home?
    a) Lancashire
    b) Northumberland
    c) Yorkshire

EASY

Answers to Quiz 28: Team Sponsors

1. Bicycle manufacture
2. Car rental
3. Telecoms
4. Online credit
5. Lottery
6. Mobile-phone operation
7. Bicycle manufacture
8. Chemicals
9. Soy-food production
10. Electronics retail
11. Oil
12. Banking
13. Metal manufacture
14. GPS manufacture
15. Camping holidays
16. Wine
17. Cycling clothing
18. Soft drinks
19. Clothes
20. Frozen foods

Quiz 30: Track World Championships

1. Which British Olympic gold medallist won the Men's Keirin at the 2013 World Championships?

2. True or false – despite his Olympic success, Chris Boardman never won a World Championship gold?

3. Which British city hosted the Track World Championships for the first time in 1996?

4. The World Championship Men's Madison is run over how many laps of the track?

5. Which pair of road stars won gold on the track in the Men's Madison at the 2008 World Championships?

6. The Men's World Championship Individual Pursuit is raced over how many metres?

7. Which BMX world champion partnered Victoria Pendleton to gold in the Women's Team Sprint at the 2008 World Championships?

8. Which two British women won individual gold at the 2012 World Championships?

9. How long in kilometres is the Men's World Championship Points Race?

10. The Women's Scratch Race is raced over how many laps of the track?

11. In the Points Race, points are awarded in sprints that take place every how many laps?

12. Which 20-year-old from Bury in Lancashire was the surprise winner of the Points Race at the 2013 World Championships?

13. Which country will host the 2014 Track World Championships?

14. The Women's Points Race is run over a course of how many kilometres?

EASY

15. Which Australian set the record for the Women's 500m Time Trial at the 2012 World Championships?

16. Over how many metres is the Women's World Championship Individual Pursuit raced?

17. Which Welsh woman won gold in the Keirin and Sprint at the 2013 World Championships?

18. Which country topped the medal table at the 2013 Track World Championships?

19. In which event did Sir Chris Hoy not win World Championship gold?
    a) keirin b) sprint c) team pursuit

20. The 2012 Track World Championships featured how many separate events?
    a) six b) eight c) ten

Answers to Quiz 29: Pot Luck

1. October
2. Kazakhstan
3. 1990
4. Bunch sprint
5. Eddy Merckx
6. Jeremy Hunt
7. Daniel Martin
8. Sean Kelly
9. Peter Sagan
10. Nissan
11. Rui Costa
12. True
13. Greg LeMond
14. Gino Bartali and Fausto Coppi
15. Michael Rogers
16. Bobby Julich
17. Chris Boardman
18. Tour de l'Avenir
19. 7,500
20. Lancashire

Quiz 31: Pot Luck

1. Who was the first native English-speaker to win Paris–Roubaix?

2. True or false – during a particularly steamy southern stage of the Tour de France, around half the field took a dip in the Mediterranean midway through the race?

3. Which Swiss rider won the E3 Harelbeke for the third time in 2013?

4. In the Tour de France, a rider is given the same finishing time as the group to which they belonged if they crash within how many kilometres of the finish?

5. Who won the Vélo d'Or award in 2012?

6. Who was left with 37 shotgun pellets in his body after a 1987 hunting accident?

7. The Passo Pordoi is the most commonly visited mountain in which race?

8. Which world-famous scientist said, 'Life is like riding a bicycle. In order to keep your balance, you must keep moving'?

9. Daniel Martin is the nephew of which famous rider?

10. Which rider rode with a picture of Pamela Anderson on his handlebars, in theory to boost his testosterone levels?

11. Which was the only 2013 UCI Pro Tour team that wore primarily orange jerseys?

12. Which Portuguese rider won the Tour de Suisse in 2013?

13. Which reigning world champion won a stage of the Giro d'Italia in 2010?

14. In the Tour de France, the 'maillot vert' is worn by the leader of which competition?

15. In which mountain range is the Col du Tourmalet?

16. Louis Joseph are the middle names of which cycling legend?

17. Which former winner turned up for the opening prologue of the 1989 Tour de France 2m 40s late?

18. What was the top-rated pro team in 2012 according to the UCI rankings?

19. Europe's largest bike race, the Vattenfall Cyclassics, is based in which city?
    a) Amsterdam b) Brussels c) Hamburg

20. Which of the following countries has the Tour de France visited?
    a) Ireland b) Scotland c) Wales

EASY

Answers to Quiz 30: Track World Championships

1. Jason Kenny
2. False
3. Manchester
4. 200
5. Mark Cavendish and Sir Bradley Wiggins
6. 4,000m
7. Shanaze Reade
8. Victoria Pendleton and Laura Trott
9. 40km
10. 40
11. Ten
12. Simon Yates
13. Colombia
14. 25km
15. Anna Meares
16. 3,000m
17. Becky James
18. Great Britain
19. Team pursuit
20. Ten

Quiz 32: Nicknames

Which rider has the following nickname?

1. The Manx Missile

2. The Lion King

3. The Badger

4. The Cannibal

5. The Professor

6. The Tashkent Terror

7. Il Diablo (The Devil)

8. Perico

9. Jaja

10. Cuddles

11. El Pistolero

12. Spartacus

13. Big Mig

14. Ale-Jet

15. The Pirate

16. Freckle

17. The God of Thunder

18. Il Campionissimo (Champion of Champions)

19. Der Kaiser

20. The Banana with the Sideburns

Answers to Quiz 31: Pot Luck

1. Sean Kelly
2. True
3. Fabian Cancellara
4. 3km
5. Sir Bradley Wiggins
6. Greg LeMond
7. Giro d'Italia
8. Albert Einstein
9. Stephen Roche
10. Mario Cipollini
11. Euskaltel-Euskadi
12. Rui Costa
13. Cadel Evans
14. Points
15. Pyrenees
16. Eddy Merckx
17. Pedro Delgado
18. Team Sky
19. Hamburg
20. Ireland

Quiz 33: Pot Luck

1. Which British rider won the Tour de Romandie in 2013?

2. Who holds the record for the most starts in the Tour de France by an Irishman?

3. Which Tour de France veteran won Olympic medals on the track for Australia in both 1992 and 1996?

4. The bugbear of many a rider, what is the French 'un pneu crevé' in English?

5. Who is the only rider to finish either first or second in every Tour de France he completed?

6. Who was the first rider to win the Tour de France four years in a row?

7. Alberto Contador gained 39 seconds after attacking which rival who suffered mechanical trouble on a climb on stage 15 of the 2010 Tour de France?

8. The 2013 Tour de France featured how many individual time trials?

9. Which cyclist makes a cameo appearance in the book 'Asterix in Belgium'?

10. Who was the first cyclist to be named Sportsman of the Year by the American magazine 'Sports Illustrated'?

11. Sir Bradley Wiggins allowed which rival to catch up during stage 14 of the 2012 Tour de France after tacks on the road caused a puncture?

12. True or false – time bonuses were awarded to the winners of intermediate sprints during the 2013 Tour de France?

13. In road stages of the Tour de France, points in the green jersey competition are awarded to how many riders on each stage?

14. 'The Pious' was the nickname of which two-time Tour de France winner?

15. Which Italian company is famous for its blue-green coloured bikes?

16. True or false – Mario Cipollini never won the points competition in the Giro d'Italia?

17. After retiring, which Irish rider opened a sports therapy practice in Stoke-on-Trent?

18. Does the San Sebastián Classic take place before or after the Tour de France?

19. Approximately what percentage of stages in the Giro d'Italia end with a bunch sprint?
    a) 27% b) 37% c) 47%

20. What were allowed for the first time in the 1937 Tour de France?
    a) bikes with gears b) support cars c) water bottles

Answers to Quiz 32: Nicknames

1. Mark Cavendish
2. Mario Cipollini
3. Bernard Hinault
4. Eddy Merckx
5. Laurent Fignon (and Jan Janssen)
6. Djamolidine Abdoujaparov
7. Claudio Chiappucci
8. Pedro Delgado
9. Laurent Jalabert
10. Cadel Evans
11. Alberto Contador
12. Fabian Cancellara
13. Miguel Indurain
14. Alessandro Petacchi
15. Marco Pantani
16. Stuart O'Grady
17. Thor Hushovd
18. Fausto Coppi
19. Jan Ullrich
20. Bradley Wiggins

MEDIUM QUIZZES

Quiz 34: Pot Luck

1. In which city was Robert Millar born?

2. Who is the oldest rider to have won the Tour de France green jersey competition?

3. Which British TV commentator won a quartet of individual pursuit World Championships?

4. Who are the two riders to have won the Tour de France, Giro d'Italia, and World Championship Road Race in the same year?

5. Who was the last French rider to win the Tour de France green jersey?

6. In which decade was the prologue time trial introduced into the Tour de France?

7. Which Dutchman, riding for Rabobank, won the 2011 Tour of Britain?

8. Which Australian was left with a fractured skull after being mugged in Toulouse in 1999?

9. Which Irishman won the Tour of Switzerland in 1983 and 1990?

10. Who won the Critérium du Dauphiné in 2013?

11. Which multiple Tour de France winner was described as being a rider 'who can drop nobody but whom nobody can drop'?

12. True or false – Saint Lance is the patron saint of cyclists?

13. Who are the three riders to have won the Tour de France white jersey three times?

14. In which decade did national rather than sponsored trade teams last take part in the Tour de France?

15. Who broke the women's one hour record six times between 1986 and 2000?

16. Who is the only rider to have won Paris–Nice, the Tour de Romandie, Critérium du Dauphiné, and the Tour de France in the same year?

17. The Lake Taupo Cycle Challenge is a major amateur event hosted in which Commonwealth country?

18. Alex Stieda and Steve Bauer are the only riders from which country to have worn the Tour de France yellow jersey?

19. Why did Fabian Cancellara abandon the 2012 Tour de France?
    a) to attend the birth of his daughter
    b) food poisoning
    c) broken collar bone

20. During the Tour de France, riders get through approximately how many plastic bottles?
    a) 5,000
    b) 10,000
    c) 15,000

MEDIUM

Answers to Quiz 67: Anagrams

1.	Sean Kelly	11.	Francesco Moser
2.	Chris Froome	12.	Tony Rominger
3.	Daryl Impey	13.	Raymond Poulidor
4.	David Millar	14.	Roger De Vlaeminck
5.	Mark Cavendish	15.	Fredrik Kessiakoff
6.	Thomas Voeckler	16.	Victoria Pendleton
7.	Denis Menchov	17.	Freddy Maertens
8.	Tom Boonen	18.	Claudio Chiappucci
9.	André Greipel	19.	Robert Millar
10.	Laurent Jalabert	20.	Andreas Kloden

Quiz 35: Sir Bradley Wiggins

1. Wiggins was born in which famous cycling town?

2. Which team did Wiggins join on turning professional in 2001?

3. What was the name of Wiggins' father, who was also a professional bike racer?

4. In what position did Wiggins finish in the 2011 Vuelta a España?

5. Wiggins won gold at the 2008 Olympic Games in which two track events?

6. In which year did Wiggins make his Tour de France debut?

7. Wiggins won his first Individual Pursuit World Championship title in which year?

8. Wiggins is a fan of which football club?

9. How many Olympic medals has Wiggins won?

10. True or false – Wiggins won the Laureus World Sports Award for Sportsman of the Year in 2012?

11. Wiggins was made a life member of which rugby league team in 2012?

12. How old was Wiggins when he won his first Tour de France?

13. What is the name of Wiggins' wife?

14. Wiggins has teamed up with which designer label to launch a cycling fashion range?

15. Wiggins was forced to quit the 2011 Tour de France after crashing and breaking which bone?

16. What is Wiggins' middle name?

17. In which year did Wiggins win his first Olympic medal?

18. Which Classic is Wiggins' favourite race?

19. Where did Wiggins finish in his first appearance in the Tour de France?
    a) 3rd
    b) 24th
    c) 124th

20. For which of the following teams did Wiggins not ride?
    a) Cofidis
    b) Credit Agricole
    c) Lampre

MEDIUM

Answers to Quiz 34: Pot Luck

1. Glasgow
2. Alessandro Petacchi
3. Hugh Porter
4. Eddy Merckx and Stephen Roche
5. Laurent Jalabert
6. 1960s
7. Lars Boom
8. Stuart O'Grady
9. Sean Kelly
10. Chris Froome
11. Jacques Anquetil
12. False
13. Andy Schleck, Jan Ullrich, and Marco Pantani
14. 1960s
15. Jeannie Longo-Ciprelli
16. Sir Bradley Wiggins
17. New Zealand
18. Canada
19. To attend the birth of his daughter
20. 15,000

Quiz 36: Pot Luck

1. Who was the last rider to win the Tour de France and the World Championship Road Race in the same year?

2. Which Spaniard won the 1973 Tour de France despite being knocked over by a dog on the opening stage?

3. What colour jersey does the leader wear in Tirreno–Adriatico?

4. Which French word describes the officials who ensure that teams and riders stick to the rules in the Tour de France?

5. True or false – in his first ten Grand Tour appearances Vincenzo Nibali never finished lower than 20th?

6. François Faber was the first rider from which country to win the Tour de France?

7. Is the Col d'Izoard in the Alps or the Pyrenees?

8. Who was the first rider to win the Tour de France three years in a row?

9. Jason Kenny is from which Lancashire town?

10. Who suffered a fractured elbow in the Alps while wearing yellow in the 2010 Tour de France?

11. Andy Rihs is the benefactor of which professional team?

12. Which Belgian was the top-rated cyclist of 2011 according to the UCI rankings?

13. True or false – 1928 Tour de France winner Nicolas Frantz completed a stage of the race riding a women's bicycle?

14. What is the name of Stephen Roche's brother who also once rode in the Tour de France?

15. Odile Defraye was the first rider from which country to win the Tour de France?

16. What colour jersey is worn by the leader of the King of the Mountains competition in the Tour of Switzerland?

17. Which climber was denied a stage victory at Guzet Neige in 1988 after being sent in the wrong direction by a policeman shortly before the finish?

18. Which trade team wore the famous white jersey with a chequered black band?

19. What was animal-related nickname of Julien Moineau?
    a) the bulldog
    b) the parrot
    c) the sparrow

20. For how many days did Bradley Wiggins wear the yellow jersey during the 2012 Tour de France?
    a) 9
    b) 11
    c) 13

MEDIUM

Answers to Quiz 35: Sir Bradley Wiggins

1. Ghent
2. Linda McCartney
3. Gary
4. Third
5. Individual Pursuit and Team Pursuit
6. 2006
7. 2003
8. Liverpool
9. Seven
10. False
11. Wigan Warriors
12. 32
13. Catherine
14. Fred Perry
15. Collar bone
16. Marc
17. 2000
18. Paris–Roubaix
19. 124th
20. Lampre

Quiz 37: Tour de France part 1

1. Who was the first man to win the Tour de France five times?

2. Which British rider crashed out of the 1998 Tour while wearing the yellow jersey?

3. What is the French phrase for the start of each Tour de France?

4. Who was the first British rider to win a stage of the Tour de France?

5. Chris Froome made his Tour de France debut in 2008 riding for which team?

6. Which British rider's only stage win came in St Etienne in 1995?

7. Which country hosted the start of the Tour for the first and so far only time in 1998?

8. Which bank and insurance company has sponsored the yellow jersey since 1987?

9. The 2012 Tour de France started in which famous cycling city?

10. What colour number is worn by the winner of the most aggressive rider award?

11. After Paris, which city has hosted the Tour de France the most times?

12. What is the narrowest overall margin of victory in the Tour?

13. Who won that extremely narrow victory?

14. Who was the unfortunate runner-up?

15. Which chain of convenience stores sponsored the first American team to enter the Tour de France?

16. Who is the highest-placed South American finisher in the history of the Tour de France?

17. Which Tour winner claimed the best young rider competition in 1996, 1997, and 1998?

18. Who in 2011 became the first Frenchman to win the white jersey since Gilles Delion in 1990?

19. Who was the first British rider to win a Tour de France time trial?
    a) Chris Boardman
    b) Barry Hoban
    c) Sean Yates

20. In which year did the Tour de France start in London?
    a) 2006
    b) 2007
    c) 2008

MEDIUM

Answers to Quiz 36: Pot Luck

1. Greg LeMond
2. Luis Ocaña
3. Blue
4. Commissaires
5. True
6. Luxembourg
7. Alps
8. Louison Bobet
9. Bolton
10. Cadel Evans
11. BMC
12. Philippe Gilbert
13. True
14. Lawrence
15. Belgium
16. Green
17. Robert Millar
18. Peugeot
19. The sparrow
20. 13

Quiz 38: Pot Luck

1. Who was the first cyclist to win an Olympic gold medal and the Tour de France in the same year?

2. Who was the last rider to win the Tour de France and the Giro in the same year?

3. True or false – no time bonuses were allocated for stage finishes in the 2013 Tour de France?

4. What nationality is Jakob Fuglsang?

5. The Tour Down Under is traditionally held in the third week of which month?

6. Which two British riders wore the leader's jersey in the 2013 Tirreno–Adriatico?

7. Olympic gold medallist Peter Kennaugh is from which part of the British Isles?

8. Which team won its first Grand Tour team time trial in the 2013 Giro d'Italia?

9. True or false – more than half of the winners of Milan–San Remo have been Italian?

10. In which stage race is the leader awarded a green-and-white-striped jersey?

11. What are the two South American countries to have hosted the Road World Championships?

12. What was Laurent Jalabert's animal-related nickname?

13. Which Swiss, riding for Team HTC-Columbia, won the 2010 Tour of Britain?

14. Which diminutive climber had his leg broken in two places after he was struck by a car during the 1995 Milan–Turin race?

15. In the Tour de France prologue time trial, riders set off at intervals of how many minutes?

16. During the 1970s, who was the only British rider to finish in the top three in the Tour de France green jersey competition?

17. Which rider has spent the most days wearing the yellow jersey of the Tour de France without actually winning the race?

18. Which London railway station is the most popular location for hiring Barclays bikes?

19. The fastest ever team trial in Tour de France history was recorded in 2013 by which team?
    a) Cannondale
    b) Orica GreenEdge
    c) Team Sky

20. What was their average speed over the course?
    a) 56.8kmh
    b) 57.8kmh
    c) 58.8kmh

MEDIUM

Answers to Quiz 37: Tour de France part 1

1. Jacques Anquetil	11. Bordeaux
2. Chris Boardman	12. 8 seconds
3. Grand départ	13. Greg LeMond
4. Brian Robinson	14. Laurent Fignon
5. Barloworld	15. 7-Eleven
6. Max Sciandri	16. Fabio Parra
7. Republic of Ireland	17. Jan Ullrich
8. LCL (Le Credit Lyonnais)	18. Pierre Rolland
9. Liège	19. Sean Yates
10. Red	20. 2007

Quiz 39: Giro d'Italia

1. Who holds the record for the most stage wins in the Giro?

2. What colour jersey is awarded to the best young rider in the Giro?

3. Who was the first British rider to wear the leader's jersey in the Giro d'Italia?

4. Who won the Mountains competition in the 2013 Giro?

5. Who were the two former Tour de France winners who started the 2013 Giro?

6. Which Team Sky rider finished as the best rider aged under 25 at the 2012 Giro?

7. Who were the six British riders that started the 2013 Giro?

8. Up to and including the 2013 race, which British rider has started the Giro the most times?

9. Who was the first Spaniard to win the Giro?

10. Who was disqualified from the 1999 Giro on the penultimate day of the race while in the lead?

11. Which Italian, who won the World Road Race Championship in 1977, holds the record for the most Giro time trial wins with 12?

12. Which British Giro debutant won the 2013 individual time trial from Gabicce Mare to Saltara?

13. The 1996 Giro started in which historic European capital?

14. Who in 2010 became the first native English-speaker to win the points competition at the Giro?

15. Which rider has spent the most days in the leader's jersey throughout the history of the Giro?

16. Aged just 20 years, 8 months, who in 1940 became the youngest winner of the Giro?

17. The 2013 race finished in which northern Italian city?

18. The jersey awarded to the leader of the Giro takes its colour from what newspaper?

19. How many riders started the 2013 Giro?
    a) 189
    b) 198
    c) 207

20. The 2013 Giro started from which city?
    a) Milan
    b) Naples
    c) Genoa

MEDIUM

Answers to Quiz 38: Pot Luck

1. Sir Bradley Wiggins
2. Marco Pantani
3. True
4. Danish
5. January
6. Mark Cavendish and Chris Froome
7. Isle of Man
8. Team Sky
9. False
10. Volta a Catalunya
11. Colombia and Venezuela
12. The panda
13. Michael Albasini
14. Marco Pantani
15. One minute
16. Barry Hoban
17. Fabian Cancellara
18. Waterloo
19. Orica GreenEdge
20. 57.8kmh

Quiz 40: Pot Luck

1. Who was the first rider to successfully defend an individual pursuit title at the Olympics?

2. Who is the only Irishman to have won more than one stage of the Giro d'Italia?

3. Which Colombian won the Best Young Rider competition at the 2013 Giro d'Italia?

4. Who was the first rider to win the points competition in all three Grand Tours?

5. Which American claimed his first major stage race victory after taking the honours in the 2013 Tour of California?

6. In which country was David Millar born?

7. At 22 years, which Australian time-trial specialist was the youngest competitor in the 2013 Giro d'Italia?

8. True or false – Colombian drug lord Pablo Escobar bankrolled a pro cycling team in the 1980s?

9. Which Australian was the first winner of the Tour Down Under?

10. The ochre jersey is worn by the leader of which race?

11. Which annual race always ends in the city of San Benedetto del Tronto?

12. Which country topped the medal table in cycling events at the 2010 Commonwealth Games?

13. Which multiple Classic winner was nicknamed 'The Beast of Eeklo'?

14. VCL are the initials of which famous British bike club?

Answers – page 85

15. The Argus, the largest competitive bike race in the world, takes place in which country?

16. Which American, who rides for the BMC team, won the under-23 Time Trial at the 2010 World Championships?

17. How tall is Sir Bradley Wiggins?

18. The climb of Puy de Dôme is in which mountainous region of France?

19. The slowest ever Tour de France winner took approximately how long to complete the race?
a) 238 hours b) 248 hours c) 258 hours

20. In which year were helmets made compulsory in professional road races?
a) 2001 b) 2002 c) 2003

MEDIUM

Answers to Quiz 39: Giro d'Italia

1. Mario Cipollini
2. White
3. Mark Cavendish
4. Stefano Pirazzi
5. Sir Bradley Wiggins and Cadel Evans
6. Rigoberto Urán
7. David Millar, Adam Blythe, Steve Cummings, Alex Dowsett, Mark Cavendish, Sir Bradley Wiggins
8. Charly Wegelius
9. Miguel Indurain
10. Marco Pantani
11. Francesco Moser
12. Alex Dowsett
13. Athens
14. Cadel Evans
15. Eddy Merckx
16. Fausto Coppi
17. Brescia
18. La Gazzetta dello Sport
19. 207
20. Naples

Quiz 41: Mark Cavendish

1. Cavendish won gold at the 2006 Commonwealth Games representing which team?

2. In which year did Cavendish win the Tour de France green jersey competition for the first time?

3. How many stages did Cavendish win during the 2013 Giro d'Italia?

4. In 2006, Cavendish made his professional road debut with which team?

5. Which Flanders Classic has Cavendish won for a record-equalling three times?

6. In which year did Cavendish win the World Road Race Championship?

7. In which city did he claim that Rainbow Jersey?

8. Cavendish won his first Tour de France stage riding for which team?

9. How many stages did Cavendish win during the record-breaking 2009 Tour de France?

10. Who partnered Cavendish to victory in the Madison event at the 2005 World Championships?

11. Cavendish was the overall winner of which Asian event in 2013?

12. Which single-day Classic did Cavendish win in 2009?

13. In 2009 Cavendish became the British rider with the most professional wins. Whose record did he overtake?

14. True or false – prior to taking up serious cycling, Cavendish was an aspiring ballroom dancer?

Answers – page 87

15. In which year was Cavendish born?

16. Cavendish was disqualified from stage 14 of the 2009 Tour de France after officials ruled he had pushed which rival too close to the barriers?

17. How many Olympic medals has Cavendish won?

18. Mark Cavendish was born in which town?

19. Up to and including the 2012 race, what was Cavendish's best overall finish in the Tour de France?
    a) 120th
    b) 130th
    c) 140th

20. Cavendish won his 100th career victory during which 2013 race?
    a) Giro d'Italia
    b) Paris–Nice
    c) Tour of Flanders

MEDIUM

Answers to Quiz 40: Pot Luck

1. Sir Bradley Wiggins
2. Stephen Roche
3. Carlos Betancur
4. Eddy Merckx
5. Tejay van Garderen
6. Malta
7. Luke Durbridge
8. True
9. Stuart O'Grady
10. Tour Down Under
11. Tirreno–Adriatico
12. Australia
13. Roger De Vlaeminck
14. Velo Club Londres
15. South Africa
16. Taylor Phinney
17. 6ft 3in (190cm)
18. Massif Central
19. 238 hours
20. 2003

Quiz 42: Pot Luck

1. Which former British rider has a sideline writing about scuba diving?

2. Who said, 'When I'm asked if I'm the best, I say "yes". People think that's arrogance but if they don't ask me, I don't say it'?

3. Who was the first British rider to win a stage in all three Grand Tours?

4. Who is the only Frenchman to have won the points competition in all three Grand Tours?

5. In which country does an event called 'Quebrantahuesos' take place?

6. Who are the two riders to have ridden a kilometre in less than a minute?

7. Who is Colombia's best-placed finisher in the Giro d'Italia?

8. Who is the only British woman to have won the Giro d'Italia Femminile?

9. Which future winner finished third in the 1985 Tour de France?

10. Which American won the Tour of Switzerland in 1986 and 1987?

11. The Ballon d'Alsace is a mountain in which range?

12. Chris Boardman was born in and still lives in which village on the Wirral?

13. Which American finished 4th in the 2003 Tour de France despite cracking his collarbone after crashing in the opening stage?

14. Which Dutch rider won the Women's Road World Championship in 2006 and 2012?

MEDIUM

15. In cycling, what is cadence?

16. Which Olympic gold medallist won the women's race at the 2013 London Nocturne event?

17. Which sprinter won three stages on his Grand Tour debut in the 2011 Vuelta a España?

18. Which Belgian rider famously confronted the owners of a dog that caused a crash on stage 18 of the 2012 Tour de France?

19. The great Fausto Coppi died of which disease?
    a) malaria
    b) polio
    c) tuberculosis

20. Which of these German cities has not hosted the opening stage of the Tour de France?
    a) Cologne
    b) Frankfurt
    c) Munich

MEDIUM

Answers to Quiz 41: Mark Cavendish

1. Isle of Man
2. 2011
3. Five
4. T-Mobile
5. Scheldeprijs Vlaanderen
6. 2011
7. Copenhagen
8. High Road
9. Six
10. Rob Hayles
11. Tour of Qatar
12. Milan–San Remo
13. Chris Boardman
14. True
15. 1985
16. Thor Hushovd
17. None
18. Douglas
19. 130th
20. Giro d'Italia

Quiz 43: Tour de France part 2

1. Cadel Evans won the Tour de France riding for which team?

2. Which former Olympic champion died after a terrible crash on the descent of the Col de Portet d'Aspet in 1995?

3. Which British rider's only stage win came in a time trial at Wasquehal in 1988?

4. The 2013 team time trial was staged in which resort?

5. Who won the King of the Mountains competition six times between 1971 and 1983?

6. Which perennial nearly man finished on the podium eight times, lastly at the age of 40 in 1976, but never won the Tour?

7. True or false – the first sponsor of the green jersey was a lawnmower manufacturer?

8. In 2011, who became only the second Frenchman to win a stage that culminated at Alpe d'Huez?

9. Which German sprinter won the opening stage of the 2013 Tour de France?

10. Who holds the record for the fastest ever prologue time trial in the Tour de France?

11. Which range of mountains did the Tour visit first in 2013 – the Alps or the Pyrenees?

12. Who was the only German Team Sky rider at the 2012 Tour de France?

13. What did the Tour de France do in 1954 that it had never done before?

14. Which parcel company sponsored a British team at the 1987 Tour?

15. Which Dutch rider completed a then record-breaking 16 Tours between 1970 and 1986?

16. At the age of 34 years 160 days, who in 2011 became the third oldest winner of the Tour?

17. Which German band recorded the 2003 album 'Tour de France Soundtracks'?

18. Which Briton was the youngest rider to take part in the 2007 Tour?

19. What is the maximum distance of the Tour de France?
    a) 3,400km
    b) 3,500km
    c) 3,600km

20. What is the most stages won by a rider in a single Tour de France?
    a) seven
    b) eight
    c) nine

MEDIUM

Answers to Quiz 42: Pot Luck

1. Chris Boardman
2. Mark Cavendish
3. Robert Millar
4. Laurent Jalabert
5. Spain
6. Sir Chris Hoy and Arnaud Tournant
7. Rigoberto Urán
8. Nicole Cooke
9. Stephen Roche
10. Andy Hampsten
11. Vosges Mountains
12. Hoylake
13. Tyler Hamilton
14. Marianne Vos
15. The number of revolutions of the crank per minute
16. Laura Trott
17. Peter Sagan
18. Philippe Gilbert
19. Malaria
20. Munich

Quiz 44: Pot Luck

1. Who was the last Irishman to record a top ten finish in the Tour de France?

2. Which Spaniard won the King of the Mountains at the Tour de France six times between 1954 and 1964?

3. The 2013 Critérium du Dauphiné started in which country?

4. Mark Cavendish holds the record for the most Tour de France stage wins by a British rider. Who is second on the list?

5. The climb at Gavia Pass is a feature of which race?

6. Which car manufacturer produced the bike which Chris Boardman used to win Olympic gold?

7. What role does Dr Steve Peters have with Team Sky?

8. Which sprinter, who won the World Championship Road Race in 2005 said, 'You may be champion of the world but that doesn't get you out of the washing up'?

9. The Tour de France headed to England in 1994 to mark the 50th anniversary of which event?

10. True or false – the combined length of the Tour de France courses since the race began is further than the distance between the Earth and the Moon?

11. Who in 1995 became the second oldest winner of the Giro d'Italia?

12. How many gold medals did English riders win at the 2010 Commonwealth Games?

13. What is the name of Laurent Jalabert's younger brother who rode in the Tour de France four times?

14. Which kit manufacturer produces the Tour de France's yellow jersey?

15. In 1986, who became the first French rider to win a stage at Alpe d'Huez?

16. Who won Tirreno–Adriatico for the second year in succession in 2013?

17. Which Team Sky rider finished second in the race?

18. Which New Zealander started and completed all three Grand Tours in 2009?

19. What is the animal-inspired nickname of Rein Taaramäe?
    a) the ferret
    b) the fox
    c) the frog

20. Who was the first American to compete in the Tour de France?
    a) Phil Boyer
    b) Andy Hampsten
    c) Greg LeMond

MEDIUM

Answers to Quiz 43: Tour de France part 2

1. BMC Racing
2. Fabio Casartelli
3. Sean Yates
4. Nice
5. Lucien Van Impe
6. Raymond Poulidor
7. True
8. Pierre Rolland
9. Marcel Kittel
10. Chris Boardman
11. The Pyrenees
12. Christian Knees
13. It started outside France
14. ANC
15. Joop Zoetemelk
16. Cadel Evans
17. Kraftwerk
18. Geraint Thomas
19. 3,500km
20. Eight

Quiz 45: Vuelta a España

1. Who is the only Irishman to have won the Vuelta?

2. Which Spaniards finished second and third in the 2012 race?

3. Which Swiss rider holds the record for spending the most days in the leader's jersey?

4. In 2012, who became the first Australian to win the Mountains competition?

5. Which British rider won the stage from Santiago de Compostela to Ferrol in 2012?

6. True or false – prior to the 1990s, the Vuelta traditionally started in April?

7. The 2011 race started in which resort, popular with British tourists?

8. Which Belgian won an amazing 13 stage wins during the 1977 Vuelta?

9. Which Spaniard won the race in 2011 by a margin of just 13 seconds?

10. Who is the only Colombian to have won the Vuelta?

11. Which German won the points competition in 2002, 2003, and 2004?

12. Which Spanish Tour de France winner won his home tour for the first time in 1985?

13. Between 1985 and 2012, who was the only Frenchman to win the Vuelta?

14. True or false – a plain grey shirt was at one time awarded to the leader of the King of the Mountains competition?

15. Which French climber won the Mountains competition in 2008, 2009, 2010, and 2011?

16. Which Briton wore the leader's jersey for three days during the 2001 race?

17. Who completed a clean sweep in 1995, winning the overall race as well as the Points and Mountains competitions?

18. Which American, riding for Astana, was runner-up in the 2008 Vuelta?

19. In which year did Alexandre Vinokourov win his only Vuelta?
    a) 2004
    b) 2005
    c) 2006

20. The 2009 Vuelta started in which country?
    a) Belgium
    b) Germany
    c) The Netherlands

MEDIUM

Answers to Quiz 44: Pot Luck

1. Stephen Roche
2. Federico Bahamontes
3. Switzerland
4. Barry Hoban
5. Giro d'Italia
6. Lotus
7. Psychiatrist and Head of Medicine
8. Tom Boonen
9. D-Day
10. True
11. Tony Rominger
12. None
13. Nicolas Jalabert
14. Le Coq Sportif
15. Bernard Hinault
16. Vincenzo Nibali
17. Chris Froome
18. Julian Dean
19. The fox
20. Phil Boyer

Quiz 46: Pot Luck

1. Who are the two riders to have won at least three stages in five consecutive Tours de France?

2. In which country was Chris Froome born?

3. The track race known as the Madison takes its name from a venue in which city?

4. According to a song by Katie Melua, there are how many bicycles in Beijing?

5. Which outdoor clothing manufacturer sponsored the 2013 British Tour Series?

6. True or false – Djamolidine Abdoujaparov won the points competition in all three Grand Tours?

7. What was the only Danish team to take part in the 2013 Tour de France?

8. Which Italian's career included two second places, one third place, and a King of the Mountains title in the Tour de France and two seconds, a third, fourth, and a fifth place in the Giro, as well as two Mountains and a Points title?

9. What are the first names of the four Simon brothers who rode in the Tour de France in the 1980s and 1990s?

10. Who was the last rider to win the Tour de France whose first name and surname started with the same letter?

11. Miguel Poblet, Adriano Baffi, and Alessandro Petacchi are the only three riders to have accomplished which feat?

12. Which recent Grand Tour winner won a silver medal in the World Mountain Bike Championships in 2003?

13. Who is the only Swiss rider to have won the Road World Championship Time Trial?

14. The name of which musical instrument is used to describe riding at a slow pace during a race?

15. Which opera singer sang the British national anthem in Paris after the final stage of the 2012 Tour de France?

16. Alberto Contador made his Tour de France debut in 2005 riding for which team?

17. Which team-mate of Cadel Evans overtook the Aussie in the 2012 Tour de France time trial at Chartres despite starting three minutes behind?

18. The 2013 Tour de France featured how many intermediate sprints on normal road-race days?

19. In which decade did Alpe d'Huez feature on the Tour de France route for the first time?
    a) 1950s b) 1960s c) 1970s

20. What nickname is given to the youngest rider of the Tour de France?
    a) Benjamin du Tour b) François du Tour c) Lionel du Tour

MEDIUM

Answers to Quiz 45: Vuelta a España

1. Sean Kelly
2. Alejandro Valverde and Joaquim Rodriguez
3. Alex Zulle
4. Simon Clarke
5. Steve Cummings
6. True
7. Benidorm
8. Freddy Maertens
9. Juan Jose Cobo
10. Luis Herrera
11. Erik Zabel
12. Pedro Delgado
13. Laurent Jalabert
14. True
15. David Moncoutie
16. David Millar
17. Laurent Jalabert
18. Levi Leipheimer
19. 2006
20. The Netherlands

Quiz 47: Miguel Indurain

1. In which year did Indurain win his maiden Tour de France?

2. Indurain won all of his Tour de France titles while riding for which team?

3. Indurain set the record for The Hour in 1994. Which British rider's record did he break?

4. Miguel Indurain is from which region of Spain?

5. How tall is Indurain?

6. True or false – Indurain abandoned his first Tour de France after just four stages?

7. Which East European finished second behind Indurain in the 1994 Tour de France?

8. How many times did Indurain win the Giro d'Italia?

9. True or false – Indurain never wore the polka-dot jersey at the Tour de France?

10. In which year was Indurain born?

11. Indurain won his only Rainbow Jersey in the Elite Road Time Trial hosted in which South American country?

12. Between 1991 and 1995 how many mountain stages did Indurain win in the Tour de France?

13. What was Indurain's best finish in the Vuelta a España?

14. True or false – after retiring from professional cycling Indurain became a farmer?

15. In which city did Indurain win Olympic gold?

Answers – page 99

16. What was the most number of stages that Indurain won in a single Tour de France?

17. Indurain wore the yellow jersey at the Tour de France for how many days in total?

18. In which year did Indurain make his last Tour de France appearance?

19. What was Indurain's lowest Tour de France finish?
    a) 77th
    b) 87th
    c) 97th

20. At his racing peak Indurain had a resting heart rate of how many beats per minute?
    a) 28
    b) 30
    c) 32

MEDIUM

Answers to Quiz 46: Pot Luck

1. Mark Cavendish and Bernard Hinault
2. Kenya
3. New York
4. 9 million
5. Pearl Izumi
6. True
7. Saxo-Tinkoff
8. Claudio Chiappucci
9. Pascal, Régis, Jerôme, and François
10. Jan Janssen
11. They've all won a stage in all three Grand Tours in the same year
12. Ryder Hesjedal
13. Alex Zulle
14. Piano
15. Lesley Garrett
16. Liberty Seguros
17. Tejay van Garderen
18. One
19. 1950s
20. Benjamin du Tour

Quiz 48: Pot Luck

1. Which Frenchman, who was the youngest rider in the race, won the mountain stage to Porrentruy on the 2012 Tour de France?

2. Which journalist wrote the book, 'Seven Deadly Sins: My Pursuit of Lance Armstrong'?

3. Which contemporary rider said, 'When you win sprints you prove you're a great sprinter. When you win a great one-day race, you've proved you're a great rider'?

4. Who is the only rider to have won the Tour de France and the Giro d'Italia in the same year on three occasions?

5. 'A Sunday in Hell' was a 1976 film made about which race?

6. The RadioShack-Leopard team is based in which country?

7. Who is the only British rider to have won the Volta a Catalunya?

8. Which Italian won the World Road Race Championship in 1991 and 1992?

9. Kurt Stopl was the first rider from which country to wear the Tour de France yellow jersey?

10. Which sprinter broke his collarbone just 60m from the finish line on the Champs-Elysées in the 1991 Tour de France?

11. Which Briton won the World Professional Pursuit Championship in Besançon, France in 1980?

12. Who in 1996 became the first native English-speaker to win La Flèche Wallone?

13. Who was the last man to win the Tour de France whose surname started and ended with the same letter?

14. Who won a hat-trick of road race World Championships in 1999, 2001, and 2004?

15. Which classic race was created by Karel Van Wijnendaele of the Sportwereld newspaper in 1913?

16. Which Tour de France winner adopted an Ethiopian child called Robel in 2012?

17. Why was Chris Froome disqualified from the 2010 Giro d'Italia?

18. Bjarne Riis and Jan Ullrich won the Tour de France riding for which team?

19. Which Irish rider completed the most Tours de France?
    a) Martin Earley
    b) Sean Kelly
    c) Stephen Roche

20. What was unique about Henri Cornet and his 1904 Tour de France win?
    a) he's the only teenager to win
    b) he won every stage of the race
    c) he finished second on every stage bar one

MEDIUM

Answers to Quiz 47: Miguel Indurain

1.	1991	11.	Colombia
2.	Banesto	12.	None
3.	Graeme Obree	13.	Second
4.	Navarre	14.	False
5.	6ft 2in (1.88m)	15.	Atlanta
6.	True	16.	Two
7.	Piotr Ugrumov	17.	60
8.	Twice	18.	1996
9.	False	19.	97th
10.	1964	20.	28

Quiz 49: Sir Chris Hoy

1. In which year did Hoy win his first Olympic gold medal?

2. In which event did he win his maiden Olympic gold?

3. The Sir Chris Hoy Velodrome is in which city?

4. Hoy was the recipient of how many Olympic gold medals?

5. In which year did Hoy receive his knighthood?

6. How old was Hoy when he won his first Olympic gold medal?

7. True or false – Hoy had to take his own race bike and wheels to the 1996 European Under-23 Championships in Moscow?

8. Hoy won his first Commonwealth Games gold in 2002 in which event?

9. In which city did he win that maiden Commonwealth gold?

10. True or false – Hoy has a BSc Honours in Applied Sports Science from the University of Edinburgh?

11. Who helped Hoy to the silver medal in the 1999 World Championship Sprint?

12. In which Scandinavian city did Hoy win his first World Championship gold?

13. In which year was Hoy voted BBC Sports Personality of the Year?

14. In which city was Hoy born?

15. How many Olympic medals did Hoy win in total?

16. Hoy's first cycling club in Edinburgh is also the name of which city in New Zealand?

Answers – page 103

17. How many World Championship titles did Hoy win?

18. Hoy's only Olympic silver was won in which event?

19. Hoy is a fan of which football club?
    a) Heart of Midlothian
    b) Hibernian
    c) St Mirren

20. In which country did Hoy set a world record for the 500m sprint?
    a) Belgium
    b) Bolivia
    c) Brazil

MEDIUM

Answers to Quiz 48: Pot Luck

1. Thibaut Pinot
2. David Walsh
3. Mark Cavendish
4. Eddy Merckx
5. Paris–Roubaix
6. Luxembourg
7. Robert Millar
8. Gianni Bugno
9. Germany
10. Djamolidine Abdoujaparov
11. Tony Doyle
12. Lance Armstrong
13. Bernard Thévenet
14. Oscar Freire
15. Tour of Flanders
16. Cadel Evans
17. He held onto a motorbike on a mountain stage
18. Telekom
19. Sean Kelly
20. He's the only teenager to have won the race

Quiz 50: Pot Luck

1. Prior to Cadel Evans in 2005, who was the last Australian to enjoy a Tour de France top ten finish?

2. Who was the last German rider to make the podium in the Tour de France?

3. Between 1903 and 1967 the Tour de France finished at which famous Parisian location?

4. Which Briton was the Individual Pursuit world champion in 1993 and 1995?

5. True or false – Peter Sagan won the Slovak Cup while riding a bike borrowed from his sister?

6. Which fishy sounding Frenchman won the Best Young Rider competition at the 1999 Tour de France?

7. What is the name of Roger de Vlaeminck's brother who was also a professional cyclist?

8. Which famous Tour de France climb is nicknamed the 'Giant of Provence'?

9. For how many stages did Cadel Evans wear the yellow jersey during the 2011 Tour de France?

10. Which rider enjoyed the nickname 'Mr Paris–Nice'?

11. In which year did Mark Cavendish make his Tour de France debut?

12. Which race features a climb called Bonny Doon?

13. How many times did Eddy Merckx ride the Tour de France?

14. Which famous Alpine climb features memorials commemorating Louison Bobet and Fausto Coppi?

15. Which Spanish island hosted the 2007 Track World Championships?

16. Which reigning world champion won seven stages of the Giro d'Italia in 1977?

17. How did a 30-year-old actor called Xavier Clement make headlines on the final stage of the 1997 Tour de France?

18. Who was the last rider to win the King of the Mountains at the Giro d'Italia whose first name and surname start with the same letter?

19. In which year did the first British Tour Series take place?
    a) 2008
    b) 2009
    c) 2010

20. What name is given to the day of a multi-stage race that contains the highest point of the race?
    a) King Stage
    b) Prince Stage
    c) Queen Stage

Answers to Quiz 49: Sir Chris Hoy

1. 2004	11. Craig MacLean and Jason Queally
2. 1km Time Trial	12. Copenhagen
3. Glasgow	13. 2008
4. Six	14. Edinburgh
5. 2009	15. Seven
6. 28	16. Dunedin
7. True	17. 11
8. 1km Time Trial	18. Team Sprint
9. Manchester	19. Heart of Midlothian
10. True	20. Bolivia

MEDIUM

Quiz 51: Classics

1. Which race is sometimes known as 'The Queen of the Classics'?

2. Who in 2006 became the first Spaniard to win Liège–Bastogne–Liège then won again in 2008?

3. Which race was Tom Boonen describing when he said, 'This race is all about surviving, surviving, surviving'?

4. A climb called the Poggio is a feature of which Classic?

5. Who are the three riders, all Belgians, to have won all five of 'The Monuments'?

6. True or false – no Spanish rider has ever won Paris–Roubaix?

7. On which day of the week does Gent–Wevelgem take place?

8. Which Italian in 2004 became the first rider to win the Amstel Gold Race, Flèche Wallonne, and Liège–Bastogne–Liège in the same season?

9. Who was the first Australian to win Paris–Roubaix?

10. A Spanish rider won the Giro di Lombardia for the first time in 2012. Which one?

11. With seven victories, who has won Milan–San Remo the most times?

12. Who won the E3 Harelbeke four years on the trot between 2004 and 2007?

13. First staged in 1892, what is cycling's oldest classic?

14. Alexandre Vinokourov is one of two Kazakh riders to have won Liège–Bastogne–Liège. Who is the other?

15. In 2004, who became the first (and so far only) Swedish rider to win Paris–Roubaix?

16. Who lost the 2004 Milan–San Remo to Oscar Freire because he lifted his arms to celebrate too early?

17. In 2011, who became the first Australian to win Milan–San Remo?

18. Which fellow Aussie won Milan–San Remo a year later?

19. What is the longest one-day Classic?
    a) Liège–Bastogne–Liège
    b) Milan–San Remo
    c) Paris–Roubaix

20. How long is this gruelling race?
    a) 278km
    b) 288km
    c) 298km

MEDIUM

Answers to Quiz 50: Pot Luck

1. Phil Anderson
2. Andreas Kloden
3. Parc des Princes
4. Graeme Obree
5. True
6. Benoît Salmon
7. Erik
8. Mont Ventoux
9. One
10. Sean Kelly
11. 2008
12. Tour of California
13. Seven
14. Col d'Izoard
15. Majorca
16. Freddy Maertens
17. He streaked along the Champs-Elysées
18. Claudio Chiappucci
19. 2009
20. Queen Stage

Quiz 52: Pot Luck

1. Which Classic is known as the 'Race of the Falling Leaves'?

2. What nationality is Team Katusha rider Simon Špilak?

3. Who was the last rider to win the Giro d'Italia whose surname starts and ends with the same letter?

4. Who is the only American rider to win one of cycling's five 'Monuments'?

5. 'Titi' was the nickname of which Tour de France prologue specialist?

6. Who in 2012 became the first rider born in the 1990s to win a stage of the Tour de France?

7. Days later, which Frenchman became the second rider born in the 1990s to achieve the feat?

8. True or false – before taking to the track, Sir Chris Hoy was a Scottish champion BMX rider?

9. What nationality is Yauheni Hutarovich?

10. 'Nanard' was the nickname of which Tour de France winner from the 1970s?

11. The Tour de l'Avenir is a race for riders under what age?

12. What was the name of the fly-on-the-wall documentary that followed the fortunes of the British Olympic team and Team Sky during the 2012 season?

13. Which company sponsored Britain's Tour Series from 2010 until 2012?

14. Which multiple Tour de France green jersey winner became a sprint adviser to Team Katusha after retiring from competitive racing?

15. Who has more Grand Tour stage victories – Tom Boonen or Thor Hushovd?

16. Which American youngster was runner-up in the 2013 edition of Paris–Nice?

17. Which Tour de France winner is a supporter of the freedom for Tibet movement and wore a Tibetan flag on his base layer during the 2008 Tour?

18. 'Gule førertrøje' is the name for the yellow jersey in which language?

19. Which of the following riders did not win the Tour de France on their first appearance in the race?
a) Bernard Hinault b) Greg LeMond c) Eddy Merckx

20. Irish rider Daniel Martin was born in which English city?
a) Birmingham b) London c) Manchester

MEDIUM

Answers to Quiz 51: Classics

1. Paris–Roubaix
2. Alejandro Valverde
3. Paris–Roubaix
4. Milan–San Remo
5. Roger De Vlaeminck, Rik Van Looy, and Eddy Merckx
6. True
7. Sunday
8. Davide Rebellin
9. Stuart O'Grady
10. Joaquim Rodríguez
11. Eddy Merckx
12. Tom Boonen
13. Liège–Bastogne–Liège
14. Maxim Iglinsky
15. Magnus Bäckstedt
16. Erik Zabel
17. Matt Goss
18. Simon Gerrans
19. Milan–San Remo
20. 298km

Quiz 53: The 2012 Olympics

1. Who was the only British rider to win a silver medal on the track at the 2012 Olympic Games?

2. Who controversially crashed during a heat of the Men's Sprint against Germany?

3. Who was Britain's first medal winner in any sport at the London 2012 Olympics?

4. Which Dutch rider won the Women's Road Race?

5. Who was the only Team GB track cyclist to miss out on a medal in 2012?

6. Which Frenchman finished second in the Men's Individual Sprint at London 2012?

7. Excluding Great Britain, which country won the most track medals at London 2012?

8. Which former world champion was well placed in the leading group in the Men's Road Race but crashed with 15km to go?

9. Whom did Sir Chris Hoy beat in the final of the Men's Keirin?

10. Who won the silver medal in the 2012 Men's Road Race?

11. Which British pair were disqualified from the Women's Team Sprint after an illegal overtake in their semi-final victory over Ukraine?

12. Which German collected a silver medal in the Men's Individual Road Time Trial?

13. At the age of 20 years and 102 days, who became the youngest ever Olympic cycling gold medalist in 2012?

14. Which Australian's record did she beat?

15. Who was Britain's only representative in the Women's BMX final?

16. Sir Paul McCartney led a spontaneous rendition of which song after the final of the Women's Team Pursuit?

17. Which American won gold in the Women's Individual Road Time Trial?

18. What nationality is Mariana Pajón, the winner of the Women's BMX race?

19. Who was Britain's best-placed finisher in the Women's Road Time Trial?
    a) Lizzie Armitstead b) Emma Pooley c) Laura Trott

20. Over what distance was the Men's Road Individual Time Trial contested?
    a) 33km b) 44km c) 55km

Answers to Quiz 52: Pot Luck

1. Giro di Lombardia
2. Slovenian
3. Tony Rominger
4. Tyler Hamilton
5. Thierry Marie
6. Peter Sagan
7. Thibaut Pinot
8. True
9. Belarussian
10. Bernard Thévenet
11. 23

12. British Cycling: Road to Glory
13. Halfords
14. Erik Zabel
15. Thor Hushovd
16. Andrew Talansky
17. Cadel Evans
18. Danish
19. Greg LeMond
20. Birmingham

MEDIUM

Quiz 54: Pot Luck

1. The climb of the Cipressa is a feature of which one-day Classic?

2. The 2012 UCI BMX World Championships were hosted in which British city?

3. How many of the five one-day 'Monuments' did Miguel Indurain win?

4. The cobbled climb of the Paterberg is a feature of which one-day classic?

5. 'The Hammer' was the nickname of which Grand Tour winner from the 1990s?

6. True or false – Eddy Merckx won the World Men's Elite Cyclo-cross Championship?

7. In which language is the yellow jersey known as the 'Gelbe Trikot'?

8. Who is the only rider to have won each of the one-day 'Monuments' more than once?

9. Does the Tour de l'Avenir feature trade teams or national teams?

10. Former World Champion Oscar Freire spent his final season on the road with which team?

11. Which veteran led his Motorpoint-Marshalls Pasta team to victory in the 2010 British Tour Series?

12. 'Ete' was the nickname of which prolific sprinter?

13. Who was appointed general manager to Team Astana in December 2012?

14. Which Colombian rider was named after the author of 'Les Misérables'?

15. Which Tour de France winner is also a breeder of canaries and finches?

16. Who was the last Belgian-born winner of the Tour de France?

17. Eddy Merckx was one of two Belgians to win the Tour de France in the 1970s. Who was the other?

18. Which US president said, 'Nothing compares to the simple pleasure of a bike ride'?

19. Which of these riders spent two years working in a bank after he left school?
    a) Mark Cavendish
    b) Sir Chris Hoy
    c) Sir Bradley Wiggins

20. To what does 'La Flèche Wallone' translate in English?
    a) The Walloon Arrow
    b) The Walloon Kite
    c) The Walloon Triangle

MEDIUM

Answers to Quiz 53: The 2012 Olympics

1. Victoria Pendleton
2. Philip Hindes
3. Lizzie Armitstead
4. Marianne Vos
5. Jess Varnish
6. Gregory Bauge
7. Australia
8. Fabian Cancellara
9. Maximilian Levy
10. Rigoberto Urán
11. Victoria Pendleton and Jess Varnish
12. Tony Martin
13. Laura Trott
14. Anna Meares
15. Shanaze Reade
16. Hey Jude
17. Kristin Armstrong
18. Colombian
19. Emma Pooley
20. 55km

Quiz 55: Olympic Cycling

1. Which country won a surprise gold in the Women's Sprint at London 2012?

2. Which three events that featured at the 2008 Olympics were scrapped for 2012?

3. Which future winner won silver in the Men's Road Race in 2000?

4. True or false – cycling appeared in the very first Olympic Games in 1896?

5. Which British pair failed to win a medal in the Madison event at the 2008 Games?

6. Who was Britain's only gold-medal-winning cyclist at the 2000 Games in Sydney?

7. After Sir Bradley Wiggins and Sir Chris Hoy, who is Britain's most successful cycling Olympian with four medals, three gold and a silver?

8. Which British rider won silver behind Sir Chris Hoy in the 2008 Men's Keirin?

9. Who won the 2008 Men's Olympic Road Time Trial?

10. True or false – an Australian BMX rider changed his name by deed poll to Kamikazi prior to the 2008 Games in Beijing?

11. Who were the three members of the British sprint team that won gold at the 2008 Olympics?

12. Which British rider won bronze in the Men's Road Race in Atlanta in 1996?

13. What is the penultimate event of a Men's Olympic Omnium?

14. Which Briton won the silver medal in the Women's Time Trial at the 2008 Games?

15. Which German, who shares his name with a former Arsenal goalkeeper, won four Olympic track medals between 1992 and 2000?

16. In which year was the last Olympic Games when Britain failed to win a cycling gold medal?

17. Which Briton finished second behind Sir Chris Hoy in the 2008 Individual Sprint?

18. Who won silver in the Women's Individual Pursuit at the Beijing Games?

19. How many gold medals did the Great Britain team win in Beijing in 2008?
    a) 7 b) 8 c) 9

20. David Weller is the only Olympic cycling medallist from which country?
    a) Jamaica b) South Africa c) Zimbabwe

MEDIUM

Answers to Quiz 54: Pot Luck

1. Milan–San Remo	11. Malcolm Elliott
2. Birmingham	12. Erik Zabel
3. None	13. Alexander Vinokourov
4. Tour of Flanders	14. Victor Hugo Peña
5. Tony Rominger	15. Alberto Contador
6. False	16. Sir Bradley Wiggins
7. German	17. Lucien Van Impe
8. Eddy Merckx	18. John F Kennedy
9. National teams	19. Mark Cavendish
10. Team Katusha	20. The Walloon Arrow

Quiz 56: Pot Luck

1. Who in 2013 became the first Czech rider to win the one-day Amstel Gold race?

2. Juan Esteban Curuchet and Walter Fernando Perez won the Men's Madison at the 2008 Olympics representing which country?

3. Which part of London hosted a leg of the 2013 British Tour Series?

4. In which decade did motorcycle TV crews follow the Tour de France for the first time?

5. Which Russian started, and completed, 15 Tours de France between 1991 and 2006?

6. Nicolas Frantz is the only rider from which country to have won the Tour de France more than once?

7. Who in 2003 became the first British rider to win the Tour de Picardie?

8. Prior to Sir Bradley Wiggins, who was the last rider to win the Critérium du Dauphiné and the Tour de France in the same year?

9. Who was the first cyclist to win the BBC Sports Personality of the Year award?

10. What nationality is Natnael Berhane?

11. True or false – all of the riders to have won the Tour de France five times have also won the Critérium du Dauphiné?

12. Which one-day specialist was known as the 'Emperor of Herentals'?

13. In what language is the yellow jersey known as the 'gele trui'?

14. Which Tour de France winner secretly helped the Italian resistance during the Second World War?

15. Who was the first Tour de France winner who was unable to defend his title the following year because of a doping violation?

16. In French, what is referred to as 'un jour sans'?

17. Which rider was the subject of the acclaimed 1974 documentary 'La Course en Tête'?

18. Which Tour de France winner died in 1960 while on a racing and hunting trip to what is now Burkina Faso in Africa?

19. Alberto Contador was born in which Spanish city?
a) Barcelona b) Madrid c) Valencia

20. What was the nickname of early Tour de France winner Maurice Garin?
a) The Butcher b) The Chimney-sweep c) The Undertaker

MEDIUM

Answers to Quiz 55: Olympic Cycling

1. Germany
2. Individual Pursuit, Madison, and the Points Race
3. Alexander Vinokourov
4. True
5. Sir Bradley Wiggins and Mark Cavendish
6. Jason Queally
7. Jason Kenny
8. Ross Edgar
9. Fabian Cancellara
10. True
11. Sir Chris Hoy, Jason Kenny, and Jamie Staff
12. Max Sciandri
13. 15km Scratch Race
14. Emma Pooley
15. Jens Lehmann
16. 1996
17. Jason Kenny
18. Wendy Houvenaghel
19. 8
20. Jamaica

Quiz 57: Paris–Nice

1. Who in 2013 became the first Australian to win Paris–Nice?

2. In which month is Paris–Nice traditionally run?

3. Which Frenchman won a hat-trick of Paris–Nice races in 1995, 1996, and 1997?

4. Which HTC-Highroad rider won the race in 2011?

5. Who is the only Frenchman to have won the race five times?

6. Who in 1981 became the first Irish rider to win the race?

7. Who are the two Swiss riders to have won Paris–Nice?

8. In 2005, who became the first American winner of Paris–Nice?

9. Who made it an American one-two after winning the race a year later in 2006?

10. Who are the two Britons to have won the race?

11. Which Tour de France legend won the race by just 8 seconds in 1990?

12. Which Belgian won six stages during the 1976 race?

13. Who, with wins in 2002 and 2003, was the last rider to win Paris–Nice in consecutive years?

14. Which Kazakh rider was killed following a crash in the 2003 race?

15. Who holds the record for the most stage wins in Paris–Nice with 21?

16. Which Italian beat Rinaldo Nocentini by just 3 seconds to win the race in 2008?

17. Which British rider finished 151st out of 151 in the 2013 race?

18. Including the prologue, Paris–Nice comprises how many stages?

19. Alphonse Schepers, the first winner of Paris–Nice, was from which country?
    a) Belgium
    b) France
    c) Netherlands

20. In which year did the race take place for the first time?
    a) 1923
    b) 1933
    c) 1943

MEDIUM

Answers to Quiz 56: Pot Luck

1. Roman Kreuziger
2. Argentina
3. Canary Wharf
4. 1950s
5. Viatcheslav Ekimov
6. Luxembourg
7. David Millar
8. Miguel Indurain
9. Tommy Simpson
10. Eritrean
11. True
12. Rik Van Looy
13. Dutch
14. Gino Bartali
15. Marco Pantani
16. A bad day
17. Eddy Merckx
18. Fausto Coppi
19. Madrid
20. The Chimney-sweep

Quiz 58: Pot Luck

1. On which day of the week does Milan–San Remo take place?

2. What is the second discipline in a Men's Olympic Omnium?

3. Which race covers a longer distance – Paris–Nice or Tour Down Under?

4. Who won back-to-back Critérium du Dauphiné titles in 2008 and 2009?

5. True or false – nobody whose surname starts with a vowel has ever won the King of the Mountains at the Tour de France?

6. Who experienced bleeding in his brain caused by a congenital condition known as cerebral cavernoma during the 2004 Vuelta a Asturias?

7. True or false – the winner of the Tour de France is allowed to wear the yellow jersey on the opening stages of the following year's race?

8. 'Pitbull' is the nickname of which American Garmin rider?

9. Which Tour de France winner celebrated winning a stage and the birth of his child in 2003 by sticking a baby's dummy in his mouth when crossing the finish line?

10. Which Danish rider spent 881km in breakaways during the 2012 Tour de France but failed to win a single stage?

11. Which pair, one Spanish, the other Portuguese, exchanged blows after a controversial stage of the 2010 Tour de France?

12. In 1991, Mauro Ribeiro became the first rider from which country to win a stage of the Tour de France?

13. Which noted rider was born with the surname Gunderson?

Answers – page 121

14. In the Tour de France, for what is the Souvenir Henri Desgrange prize awarded?

15. Who in 2012 became the youngest rider to enjoy an overall top ten finish in the Tour de France since 1947?

16. The 2010 documentary 'Chasing Legends' followed the fortunes of which professional team?

17. Bbox Bouygues Telecom is the former name of which team?

18. Who in 2011 became the first American rider to win a Tour de France stage on the 4th of July?

19. How many victories did Team Sky enjoy during 2012?
    a) 27 b) 37 c) 47

20. How long was the team time trial in the 2013 Tour de France?
    a) 15km b) 25km c) 35km

MEDIUM

Answers to Quiz 57: Paris–Nice

1. Richie Porte
2. March
3. Laurent Jalabert
4. Tony Martin
5. Jacques Anquetil
6. Stephen Roche
7. Tony Rominger and Alex Zülle
8. Bobby Julich
9. Floyd Landis
10. Tommy Simpson and Sir Bradley Wiggins
11. Miguel Indurain
12. Freddy Maertens
13. Alexander Vinokourov
14. Andrey Kivilev
15. Eddy Merckx
16. Davide Rebellin
17. David Millar
18. Eight
19. Belgium
20. 1933

Quiz 59: Bernard Hinault

1. In which year did Hinault win his first Tour de France?

2. How old was Hinault when he won his first Tour de France?

3. How many Grand Tours did Hinault win in total?

4. Hinault is from which region of France?

5. True or false – Hinault finished tenth in the French Cross-Country Running Championship as a junior?

6. Hinault won his first Tour de France riding for which team?

7. Hinault was runner-up in the 1984 Tour de France. Who beat him?

8. In which year did Hinault win his only World Championship Road Race?

9. At what age did Hinault retire from professional cycling?

10. Hinault was unable to move his index and middle fingers for three weeks after winning which 'Monument' in freezing conditions?

11. True or false – after retiring, Hinault became a cattle farmer?

12. How many times did Hinault win the Giro d'Italia?

13. Which of the two 'Monuments' did Hinault fail to win?

14. How many times did Hinault win the Vuelta a España?

15. Hinault won his final Tour de France riding for which team?

16. True or false – Hinault won both the green jersey and the polka-dot jersey during his Tour de France career?

17. Who beat Hinault to the yellow jersey in the 1986 Tour de France?

18. In which year did Hinault win his last Tour de France?

19. How many stages of the Tour de France did Hinault win throughout his career?
    a) 26
    b) 27
    c) 28

20. How many of those stage wins were in time trials?
    a) 18
    b) 19
    c) 20

Answers to Quiz 58: Pot Luck

1. Saturday
2. 30km Points Race
3. Paris–Nice
4. Alejandro Valverde
5. True
6. Alberto Contador
7. True
8. Andrew Talansky
9. Carlos Sastre
10. Michael Mørkøv
11. Carlos Barredo and Rui Costa
12. Brazil
13. Lance Armstrong
14. Leading the race over the highest climb of the Tour
15. Thibaut Pinot
16. Team Columbia-High Road
17. Team Europcar
18. Tyler Farrar
19. 47
20. 25km

MEDIUM

Quiz 60: Pot Luck

1. What is the third discipline in a Men's Olympic Omnium?

2. Prior to Sir Bradley Wiggins, who was the last British rider to win the Critérium du Dauphiné?

3. Which multiple Tour de France winner was runner-up in the World Road Race Championship in 1993 and 1995?

4. Stephen Roche won the Tour de France riding for a team sponsored by which jeans manufacturer?

5. True or false – Colombian climbers Luis Herrera and Oliverio Rincon have both been kidnapped in their homeland?

6. Who are the two Spaniards to have won the Road World Championship Time Trial?

7. Who owns a bike shop called Mellow Johnny's?

8. Prior to Sir Bradley Wiggins, who was the last rider to win the Critérium du Dauphiné and Paris–Nice in the same year?

9. One of Aussie actress Nicole Kidman's first acting roles was in which bike-related film?

10. Which Tour de France winner lived as a recluse in the forests of the Ardennes for a number of years following his retirement?

11. According to American mountain biker Jake Watson, you should never use what as a brake pad?

12. Which multiple Giro d'Italia winner said, 'When I was winning, I permitted myself one sexual encounter a year'?

13. Which broadcaster was appointed Chairman of the CTC in 2007?

14. Which town in the Scottish Highlands hosted a round of the 2013 Mountain Bike World Cup?

15. What nationality is mountain bike World Champion Nino Schurter?

16. Which Paralympic great won five gold medals in swimming before switching to cycling and winning another six golds?

17. Which Czech rider won gold in the Men's Mountain Bike Cross-Country at the 2012 Olympics?

18. True or false – the 1976 Tour de France featured nine consecutive mountain stages?

19. Which of the following Tour de France winners did not win the Tour de l'Avenir?
a) Bernard Hinault b) Miguel Indurain c) Greg LeMond

20. What is the most times that the yellow jersey has changed hands during a single Tour de France?
a) nine b) ten c) eleven

MEDIUM

Answers to Quiz 59: Bernard Hinault

1. 1978
2. 23
3. Ten
4. Brittany
5. True
6. Renault-Elf-Gitane
7. Laurent Fignon
8. 1980
9. 32
10. Liège–Bastogne–Liège
11. True
12. Three times
13. Tour of Flanders and the Milan–San Remo
14. Twice
15. La Vie Claire
16. True
17. Greg LeMond
18. 1985
19. 28
20. 20 (including five Prologues)

Quiz 61: Nicknames

Which rider has the following nickname?

1. The Shark of the Strait

2. Ernie

3. El Jardinerito (The Little Gardener)

4. Dr Teeth

5. Monsieur Chrono

6. Dudu

7. The Angel of the Mountains

8. Tommeke

9. Jeff

10. The Condor of Varsseveld

11. Il Grillo (The Cricket)

12. The Little Prince of Verona

13. The Archer

14. The Norwegian Bull

15. Le Monster

Answers – page 127

16. The Eternal Second

17. The Chicken

18. The Terminator

19. The Green Bullet

20. The Eagle of Herning

Answers to Quiz 60: Pot Luck

1. Elimination Race
2. Robert Millar
3. Miguel Indurain
4. Carrera
5. True
6. Miguel Indurain and Abraham Olano
7. Lance Armstrong
8. Eddy Merckx
9. BMX Bandits
10. Charly Gaul
11. Your face
12. Alfredo Binda
13. Jon Snow
14. Fort William
15. Swiss
16. Sarah Storey
17. Jaroslav Kulhavý
18. False
19. Bernard Hinault
20. Eleven

Quiz 62: Pot Luck

1. Vincenzo Nibali is from which Italian island?

2. In a Men's Olympic Omnium, the individual pursuit element is contested over what distance?

3. Which Slovenian won the 2010 Critérium du Dauphiné?

4. Riders from which country have won the Tour de France points competition the most times?

5. Greg LeMond won his second Tour de France riding for which team?

6. True or false – a podium girl at the 2003 the Tour de France was expelled after trying to start a relationship with a rider?

7. André Greipel was inspired to take up cycling after watching which film starring Kevin Costner?

8. David Millar was brought up in which Asian country?

9. How many British riders have won the Tour de l'Avenir?

10. Which cycling-inspired film was nominated for a Best Animated Feature Oscar in 2004?

11. Which popular French rider said, 'The race is always won by a strongman. The truth comes through the pedals'?

12. Whe defied doctors orders to win the 1963 Tour de France despite suffering from a tapeworm infection?

13. Cyclists in London can use Barclays bikes for how long before they have to pay a usage charge?

14. Which motor-racing circuit hosted the road cycling events at the 2012 Paralympic Games?

15. Whom was Claudio Chiappucci describing when he said, 'You'd see him there, with that smile on his face and you couldn't tell whether he was tired, faking it, or laughing at you'?

16. The 1973 film 'Stars & Watercarriers' is a documentary about which famous race?

17. Which British rider is noted for his leopard print cycling shoes?

18. In 2003, who became the first rider from Colombia to wear the yellow jersey at the Tour de France?

19. What is the narrowest margin of victory in the history of Paris–Roubaix?
a) 1cm b) 1 inch c) 1 foot

20. Which Belgian sprinter beat Steve Bauer in the 1990 race to claim that narrow win?
a) Dirk Demol b) Eddy Planckaert c) Eric Vanderaerden

MEDIUM

Answers to Quiz 61: Nicknames

1. Vincenzo Nibali
2. Andy Hampsten
3. Luis Herrera
4. Phil Anderson
5. Jacques Anquetil
6. Jacky Durand
7. Charly Gaul
8. Tom Boonen
9. Jean-François Bernard
10. Robert Gesink
11. Paolo Bettini
12. Damiano Cunego
13. Juan Antonio Flecha
14. Thor Hushovd
15. Greg LeMond
16. Raymond Poulidor
17. Michael Rasmussen
18. Peter Sagan
19. Alejandro Valverde
20. Bjarne Riis

Quiz 63: Jacques Anquetil

1. In which year did Anquetil win his first Tour de France?

2. Anquetil was from which region of France?

3. True or false – Anquetil won the King of the Mountains competition at the Tour de France?

4. Anquetil enjoyed an epic battle in the 1964 Tour with which fellow Frenchman?

5. How many stages did Anquetil win in his Tour de France career?

6. How many of those victories came in time trials?

7. How many times did Anquetil win the Giro d'Italia?

8. Anquetil's lowest Tour de France finish was third in 1959. Who won the race thich year?

9. Which annual time trial event did Anquetil win a record nine times?

10. In which year did Anquetil win his last Tour de France?

11. How many times did Anquetil win the World Championship Road Race?

12. In which year was Anquetil born?

13. How many times did Anquetil win the Vuelta a España?

14. What was the only 'Monument' that Anquetil won?

15. What was the name of Anquetil's blonde bombshell first wife?

16. True or false – after splitting from his first wife, Anquetil went to live with the wife of his adopted son?

17. In retirement, Anquetil lived in a château formerly owned by which famous writer?

18. Anquetil died at the age of 53 of what disease?

19. In which year did Anquetil win an Olympic medal?
    a) 1948
    b) 1952
    c) 1956

20. Prior to becoming a professional cyclist, Anquetil worked in which trade?
    a) farming
    b) metalwork
    c) woodwork

MEDIUM

Answers to Quiz 62: Pot Luck

1. Sicily
2. 4000m
3. Janez Brajkovič
4. Belgium
5. ADR
6. True
7. American Flyers
8. Hong Kong
9. None
10. Belleville Rendez-vous
11. Laurent Jalabert
12. Jacques Anquetil
13. Half an hour
14. Brands Hatch
15. Miguel Indurain
16. Giro d'Italia
17. Adam Blythe
18. Victor Hugo Peña
19. 1cm
20. Eddy Planckaert

Quiz 64: Pot Luck

1. Which cycling commentator was formerly an elephant keeper at a zoo?

2. Who was the first French rider to win the Giro d'Italia?

3. What is the name of Erik Zabel's son who signed with BMC for 2014?

4. 'The Honey Badger' is the nickname of which Garmin-Sharp rider?

5. In 2010, who became the first Irish winner of the Tour of Poland?

6. The GP Ouest-France race is held in which region of France?

7. What is the only Swiss city to host the start of the Tour de France?

8. Tommy Simpson died while climbing which mountain?

9. Who was the only Scot to win a gold medal in a cycling event at the 2010 Commonwealth Games?

10. Who was the first Russian rider to wear the yellow jersey at the Tour de France?

11. Who faked a mechanical problem with his bike so he could change it for a lighter model on a steep climb in the 1963 Tour de France?

12. Who is the only rider to have won the Tour de France on both his first and last appearances in the race?

13. True or false – the 1999 Tour de France was disrupted by stinkbomb-throwing firemen?

14. During the 1988 Tour de France, all the members of which team abandoned the race in quick succession in mysterious circumstances?

15. Lauded by critics as one of the greatest films of all time, what is the English title of the 1948 Italian film 'Ladri di Biciclette'?

16. Which multiple Tour de France winner's philosophy was neatly summed up when he said, 'As long as I live and breathe, I attack'?

17. What was the first foreign country to host the opening stage of the Vuelta a España?

18. According to which multiple Grand Tour and Classic winner, 'If the training is hard, the racing is easy'?

19. Up to 2012, how many British-born riders had taken part in the Tour de France?
   a) 31 b) 61 c) 91

20. How many teams took part in Paris–Roubaix in 2013?
   a) 20 b) 22 c) 25

MEDIUM

Answers to Quiz 63: Jacques Anquetil

1.	1957	11.	None
2.	Normandy	12.	1934
3.	False	13.	Once
4.	Raymond Poulidor	14.	Liège–Bastogne–Liège
5.	16	15.	Janine
6.	11	16.	True
7.	Twice	17.	Guy de Maupassant
8.	Federico Bahamontes	18.	Stomach cancer
9.	Grand Prix des Nations	19.	1952
10.	1964	20.	Metalwork

Quiz 65: Eddy Merckx

1. In which year did Merckx win his first Tour de France?

2. Merckx won that first Tour de France riding for which Italian team?

3. True or false – Merckx also won the King of the Mountains and the Points competition in his maiden Tour victory?

4. In which year did Merckx win his first Giro d'Italia?

5. In which year was Merckx born?

6. What was Merckx's lowest place finish in the Tour de France?

7. Merckx won his final Giro d'Italia in which year?

8. True or false – Merckx won gold in the road race at the Olympic Games?

9. Who said of Merckx, 'He's the biggest cry baby in the business ... If he is beaten then it's because of a mishap'?

10. Merckx's first major victory came in 1966 in which 'Monument'?

11. How many 'Monument' wins did Merckx enjoy in total?

12. In which year did Merckx win his last Tour de France?

13. Which major classic did Merckx fail to win?

14. Merckx won the World Championship and the Tour de France in the same year twice. In which years?

15. How many times did Merckx win the Vuelta a España?

16. What is the name of Merckx's son, who is also a professional cyclist?

17. Merckx broke the world one-hour record in 1972 riding in which Central American city?

18. In which year did Merckx retire from professional cycling?

19. What was Merckx's margin of victory in his first Tour de France win?
    a) 1m 54s
    b) 7m 54s
    c) 17m 54s

20. How many victories did Merckx enjoy in his 1,585 professional race career?
    a) 425
    b) 435
    c) 445

MEDIUM

Answers to Quiz 64: Pot Luck

1. Phil Liggett
2. Jacques Anquetil
3. Rick Zabel
4. Ramunas Navardauskas
5. Dan Martin
6. Brittany
7. Basel
8. Mont Ventoux
9. David Millar
10. Eugeni Berzin
11. Jacques Anquetil
12. Fausto Coppi
13. True
14. PDM
15. The Bicycle Thieves
16. Bernard Hinault
17. Portugal
18. Eddy Merckx
19. 61
20. 25

Quiz 66: Pot Luck

1. True or false – the Spanish parliament was suspended in 1987 so that members could watch a stage of the Tour?

2. Who in 2012 was named the first member of the Giro d'Italia Hall of Fame?

3. In which decade did the first official BMX World Championships take place?

4. Which Swiss rider was penalized during the 1991 Tour de France for driving from one stage finish to the start of the next rather than flying, prompting a strike from the rest of the peloton?

5. Excluding France, which country has provided the most entrants into the Tour de France?

6. Which quotable Tour de France veteran said, 'Having things organized is for small-minded people. Genius controls chaos'?

7. With 12 top-three finishes, who has made the podium in the Tour de France's points competition the most times?

8. What is the title of the Oscar-winning 1979 coming-of-age drama that starred a Dennis Quaid as an Italian cycling-obsessed teenager?

9. Frenchman Daniel Goussaeau is credited with creating which type of cycling competition?

10. Which European country is home to more bicycles than people?

11. The most aggressive rider on a stage of the Tour of Britain is awarded what food-related prize?

12. Who spent more days wearing the Tour de France yellow jersey – Bernard Hinault or Miguel Indurain?

13. The late Tommy Simpson was born in which Yorkshire town?

14. Which former Formula One motor-racing driver won gold in the handbiking event at the 2012 Paralympic Games?

15. Who won the British Road Race Championship in 2013?

16. Which bike-loving musician designed a series of 11 special-edition bike-racks that can be found throughout New York City?

17. What is Africa's first ever UCI-registered professional Continental Circuit team?

18. 'The High Life' is a 1985 documentary about which climber?

19. Up to the end of the 2012 race, how many different riders had started the Tour de France?
    a) 2,894 b) 4,892 c) 8,492

20. Which non-European country has had the most riders take part in the Tour de France?
    a) Australia b) Colombia c) USA

MEDIUM

Answers to Quiz 65: Eddy Merckx

1. 1969	11. 19
2. Faema	12. 1974
3. True	13. Paris–Tours
4. 1968	14. 1971 and 1974
5. 1945	15. Once
6. Sixth	16. Axel
7. 1974	17. Mexico City
8. False	18. 1978
9. Barry Hoban	19. 17m 54s
10. Milan–San Remo	20. 445

Quiz 67: Anagrams

Rearrange the letters to make the name of a well-known cyclist.

1. Lanky eels

2. From his core

3. Delay my rip

4. Mad viral lid

5. Drachma knives

6. Hacker loves tom

7. Condemn hives

8. Not be mono

9. Ripe enlarged

10. Tabular renal jet

11. Forces romances

12. Try onion germ

13. Rum loopy android

14. Cranked giver mole

15. Kirk freaks offside

16. Nip a divot electron

17. Smarty defender

18. I hiccup copula acid

19. Mr liberal rot

20. Ankles adorned

MEDIUM

Answers to Quiz 66: Pot Luck

1. True
2. Eddy Merckx
3. 1990s
4. Urs Zimmerman
5. Italy
6. Jens Voigt
7. Erik Zabel
8. Breaking Away
9. Cyclo-cross
10. The Netherlands
11. A selection of cheeses
12. Bernard Hinault
13. Doncaster
14. Alex Zanardi
15. Mark Cavendish
16. David Byrne
17. MTN-Qhubeka
18. Robert Millar
19. 4,892
20. Colombia

DIFFICULT QUIZZES

Quiz 68: Pot Luck

1. What colour jersey is worn by the race leader in the Critérium du Dauphiné?

2. Prior to 2012, who were the last two riders from the same team to finish first and second in the Tour de France?

3. Which German city hosted the 2003 World Track Championships?

4. Who stepped down as coach of the French national road race team in 2013?

5. Who was the only rider to finish all three Grand Tours in 2012?

6. With a capacity of 30,000, the world's largest velodrome is in which country?

7. Who was the last rider to win the British National Road Race Championship in consecutive years?

8. Italy's Pasquale Fornara holds the record for winning which European stage race the most times?

9. Which British rider fractured his pelvis and broke his scaphoid in 2009 after a crash at Tirreno–Adriatico?

10. Which multiple Tour de France winner said, 'I raced for pleasure, the pleasure of winning, that can never be denied'?

11. Including prologues, how many Tour de France time trial stages did Eddy Merckx win?

12. Which rider took part in 14 Tours de France, won seven stages, was runner-up three times, but never wore the yellow jersey?

13. 'Les Bicyclettes de Belsize' was a number 5 hit in 1968 for which crooner?

14. Who won eight stages of the Tour de France in 1930?

15. Who was the first Russian to win a stage of the Tour de France?

16. Which Swiss Tour de France winner died in a car crash in 1964 at the age of just 39?

17. Which British rider was runner-up in the Giro d'Italia Femminile in 2011 and 2012?

18. With six wins in the 1970s, which Belgian has won Tirreno–Adriatico the most times?

19. The first ever Tour de France featured how many stages?
    a) six b) eight c) ten

20. Bradley Wiggins grew up in which part of London?
    a) Brixton b) Kilburn c) Tooting

Answers to Quiz 100: Pot Luck

1. Woking
2. Stefano Garzelli
3. Michael Rogers
4. Laurent Jalabert
5. Emilio Estevez
6. Bernard Hinault and Bernard Thévenet
7. Dirk Demol
8. Moreno Moser
9. Jeremy Hunt
10. Gary Imlach
11. Luis Ocaña
12. Hubert Opperman
13. Ronan Pensec
14. Ken Laidlaw
15. PowerBar
16. 20
17. Harrods
18. None
19. 14.9mph
20. A strike by protesting metalworkers

DIFFICULT

Quiz 69: Tour de France part 1

1. Who was the winner of the first Tour de France?

2. In 1965 the Tour de France started in which country for the first time?

3. Who was the first Irishman to wear the yellow jersey at the Tour de France?

4. What initials appear on the sleeves of the yellow jersey?

5. Who is the only rider to have won the Tour de France without winning a single stage in any Tour?

6. What feat has been achieved by Ottavio Bottecchia in 1924, Nicolas Frantz in 1928, Roman Maes in 1935, and Jacques Anquetil in 1961?

7. Who in 1986 became the first Canadian to wear the yellow jersey?

8. Excluding France, which country has the most overall Tour de France wins?

9. Which motor manufacturer has sponsored the jersey for the best young rider since 2004?

10. Which Belgian rider was 'lanterne rouge' in 2006, 2007, and 2008?

11. Which Frenchman won the prologue time trial in 1986, 1990, and 1991?

12. Which Italian time trial specialist was the first man to win the best young rider competition?

13. How many countries hosted stages of the 1992 Tour de France?

14. What is the record number of riders to wear the yellow jersey in a single Tour de France?

15. Which Belgian finished only eighth overall on the 1976 Tour despite winning a record eight stages?

16. Who in 1986 became the first Mexican racer to ride the Tour de France?

17. Who in 2006 became the the general director of the Tour de France?

18. Which former professional rider did he succeed in that role?

19. How long was the longest ever Tour de France?
    a) 5,545km b) 5,645km c) 5,745km

20. How much prize money was awarded for a stage win on the 2013 Tour?
    a) €20,500 b) €21,500 c) €22,500

Answers to Quiz 68: Pot Luck

1.	Yellow with a blue band	11.	16
2.	Bjarne Riis and Jan Ullrich	12.	Raymond Poulidor
3.	Stuttgart	13.	Engelbert Humperdinck
4.	Laurent Jalabert	14.	Charles Pelissier
5.	Adam Hansen	15.	Dmitri Konyshev
6.	South Korea	16.	Hugo Koblet
7.	Roger Hammond	17.	Emma Pooley
8.	Tour de Suisse	18.	Roger De Vlaeminck
9.	Geraint Thomas	19.	Six
10.	Bernard Hinault	20.	Kilburn

DIFFICULT

Quiz 70: Pot Luck

1. Who was the first cyclist to win the BBC Overseas Sports Personality of the Year award?

2. Who was the only member of Britain's 2008 Olympic Track Cycling team to return home without a medal?

3. Acacio Da Silva is the only rider from which country to have won a stage of the Giro d'Italia?

4. Which former cyclist and member of the Cambio Radical Party unsuccessfully tried to gain election to the Colombian senate in 2011?

5. Which British rider finished 131st overall in the 2012 Tour de France riding for the BMC team?

6. 'Txirrindu' is the word for bicycle in which language?

7. What colour jersey is worn by the King of the Mountains in Tirreno–Adriatico?

8. Which musician wrote the 2010 book 'Bicycle Diaries'?

9. The Saffron Lane velodrome was located in which British city?

10. Who was punched by a spectator in the closing stages of the 1975 Tour de France stage at Puy de Dome?

11. Who was the first rider to win the Road Race World Championship, Paris–Roubaix, and the Tour of Flanders in the same year?

12. What is the name of Miguel Indurain's brother who completed three Tours de France between 1993 and 1999?

13. Who is the oldest man to have won the Giro d'Italia?

14. Which Tour de France winner from the 1960s would douse himself in diluted vinegar and salt to protect himself from germs?

Answers – page 147

15. In 2011, who became the first British rider to win Bayern Rundfahrt?

16. Laszlo Bodrogi is the only rider from which country to have taken part in the Tour de France?

17. What is the most consecutive years that the Giro d'Italia has been won by a non-Italian?

18. Which Tour de France climb is also known as 'Casse Desert'?

19. What is the record for the most stages won by a rider in a single Giro d'Italia?
    a) 10 b) 11 c) 12

20. During the 2012 Tour de France, Sir Bradley Wiggins received a good-luck gift from Miguel Indurain. What was it?
    a) a hat b) a neckerchief c) a water bottle

Answers to Quiz 69: Tour de France part 1

1. Maurice Garin
2. Germany
3. Shay Elliott
4. HD
5. Roger Walkowiak
6. They won the first stage of the Tour and kept the yellow jersey until the end
7. Alex Stieda
8. Belgium
9. Skoda
10. Wim Vansevenant
11. Thierry Marie
12. Francesco Moser
13. Seven
14. Eight
15. Freddy Maertens
16. Raul Alcala
17. Christian Prudhomme
18. Jean-Marie Leblanc
19. 5,745km
20. €22,500

DIFFICULT

Quiz 71: Giro d'Italia

1. Who won the Giro in 1925, 1927, 1928, 1929, and 1933?

2. Between 1969 and 2009, what colour jersey was awarded to the winner of the points competition?

3. What was the first British team to take part in the Giro?

4. Up to the 2013 race, who was the last rider whose surname starts with a vowel to win the Giro?

5. Only one American has won the Giro. Name him.

6. Which Australian won the mountain competition in 2010?

7. Who led the race from start to finish in 1990?

8. The first rider over the highest peak of the Giro receives a prize named after which rider?

9. Who won an amazing nine stages during the 2004 race?

10. In 2005, which Colombian won back-to-back mountain stages with 200km and 170km breakaways?

11. Which island, the third most populous in Italy, hosted the team time trial in the 2013 race?

12. No rider wears the number 108 in the Giro in honour of which rider who died in a crash during the 3rd stage of the 2011 event?

13. Who was the first Russian to win the Giro?

14. Which city will host the start of the 2014 Giro?

15. In which year did the first Giro take place?

16. Between 1946 and 1951 the slowest rider in the race was awarded what colour jersey?

17. Who in 1971 became the first and so far only Swede to win the race?

18. Which Russian holds the record for winning the Giro at the highest average speed?

19. What caused the crash that forced Marco Pantani to retire from the 2007 Giro?
    a) a black cat
    b) a motorcyclist
    c) a policeman taking a photo

20. Excluding Italy, which country provided the most starters in the 2013 Giro d'Italia?
    a) Belgium
    b) The Netherlands
    c) Spain

Answers to Quiz 70: Pot Luck

1. Jacques Anquetil
2. Mark Cavendish
3. Portugal
4. Fabio Parra
5. Steve Cummings
6. Basque
7. Green
8. David Byrne
9. Leicester
10. Eddy Merckx
11. Tom Boonen
12. Prudencio
13. Fiorenzo Magni (in 1955)
14. Roger Pingeon
15. Geraint Thomas
16. Hungary
17. Five
18. Col d'Izoard
19. 12
20. A neckerchief

DIFFICULT

Quiz 72: Pot Luck

1. Louise Robinson was the last British rider to win a world championship in which cycling event?

2. Which Italian celebrated winning a stage on the 2001 Vuelta a España by walking across the finish line carrying his bike above his head?

3. In which language is the word for bicycle 'Fahrrad'?

4. Which gambling company has sponsored the Tour de France's green jersey since 1992?

5. Which European football team plays its home games at the 'Stade Velodrome'?

6. What was the only Welsh town to host a leg of the 2013 British Tour Series?

7. Which Olympic gold medallist took victory in that Welsh race?

8. Which Lampre-Merida rider won Bayern Rundfahrt in 2013?

9. Which Briton finished second in the race?

10. Who in 2013 said, 'I'm addicted to winning. It's that simple. Ever since I was a child, it wasn't enough to be the best I could be, I had to be the best of everyone'?

11. Which hip-hop star said, 'It's one of the worst things in the world to wake up and not see your bike where you left it'?

12. What colour jersey is worn by the King of the Mountains in the Critérium du Dauphiné?

13. In 1991, which Colombian became the last man to win the Young Rider competition at the Tour de France whose name starts and ends with the same letter?

14. Who was fined €265 for taking a swing at a rival while climbing the Col de La Core in the 2002 Tour de France?

15. Who was on the receiving end of that famous punch?

16. Which Belgian rider, later a team director, set the record for the fastest ever stage of the Giro d'Italia after winning the prologue at a speed of 58.87kph in 2001?

17. In which race does the winner receive an edible garland of flatbreads?

18. Who finished third in the 2013 Giro d'Italia?

19. The 2013 British Pro Tour Series featured how many rounds?
a) seven
b) nine
c) eleven

20. How long was the longest ever stage in the Giro d'Italia?
a) 340km
b) 390km
c) 430km

Answers to Quiz 71: Giro d'Italia

1. Alfredo Binda
2. Mauve
3. Linda McCartney
4. Miguel Indurain
5. Andy Hampsten
6. Matthew Lloyd
7. Gianni Bugno
8. Fausto Coppi
9. Alessandro Petacchi
10. Ivan Parra
11. Ischia
12. Wouter Weylandt
13. Evgeni Berzin (in 1994)
14. Belfast
15. 1909
16. Black
17. Gosta Petterson
18. Denis Menchov
19. A black cat
20. The Netherlands

DIFFICULT

Quiz 73: Vuelta a España

1. Who was the first British rider to win the points competition at the Vuelta?

2. Pedro Delgado beat which Colombian by just 35 seconds to win the 1989 race?

3. Who was the first British rider to wear the leader's jersey in the Vuelta?

4. Which three teams were awarded wildcard entries into the 2013 Vuelta?

5. Which German won four stages in 2009 en route to taking the Points jersey?

6. Which Irishman won the mountain stage to Sierra de Bejar in 2011?

7. Excluding Spain, riders from which country have won the Vuelta the most times?

8. Which two British riders won stages in the 1988 race?

9. Who are the four Colombians to have won the King of the Mountains competition?

10. Four British riders took part in the 2012 Vuelta. Chris Froome was one, who were the other three?

11. True or false – the leader's jersey was once plain white with a horizontal red stripe?

12. Which Irishman enjoyed a famous victory on the stage from Talavera de la Reina to Avila in 2009?

13. Which pair, who have both won the Vuelta, share the record for winning the points competition the most times?

DIFFICULT

14. Who was the first Briton to win a stage in the Vuelta?

15. Who are the three German riders to have won the race?

16. Which Spaniard holds the record for the most stage wins with 39, almost double that of his closest rival?

17. Two Dutch riders have won the Vuelta. Which two?

18. In 2011, who became the first Dutch rider in over 40 years to win the points competition?

19. The leader's jersey in the Vuelta was originally what colour?
    a) blue
    b) green
    c) orange

20. In which year was the Vuelta staged for the first time?
    a) 1915
    b) 1925
    c) 1935

Answers to Quiz 72: Pot Luck

1. Cyclo-cross	11. 50 Cent
2. Filippo Simeoni	12. Red with white spots
3. German	13. Alvaro Mejia
4. PMU	14. Christophe Moreau
5. Marseille	15. Carlos Sastre
6. Aberystwyth	16. Rik Verbrugghe
7. Ed Clancy	17. La Vuelta a Colombia
8. Adriano Malori	18. Cadel Evans
9. Geraint Thomas	19. Eleven
10. Mark Cavendish	20. 430km

DIFFICULT

Quiz 74: Pot Luck

1. Who won the British National Road Race Championship title for the first time in 2011?

2. The Critérium du Dauphiné is raced over how many stages?

3. 'Rower' is the word for bicycle in which language?

4. The opening leg of the 2013 British Tour Series was held in which Scottish town?

5. What nationality was Gustaaf Deloor, the first winner of the Vuelta a España?

6. Who was the first Australian to wear the leader's jerseys of all three Grand Tours?

7. Who was the leading British finisher in the 2013 Giro?

8. Which British Olympian turned road rider had his spleen removed after a training crash in Sydney in 2005?

9. Which Irishman won the Scratch race at the 2013 World Track Championships?

10. In 1947, Poland's Edouard Klabinski became the first winner of which annual stage race?

11. In which city was Aussie legend Phil Anderson born?

12. In 2011, Andrey Amador Bipkazacova became the first rider from which country to take part in the Tour de France?

13. In the 2013 British Tour Series, each race featured how many riders from each team?

14. Who became the second Briton to win the Tour de Picardie in 2010?

15. What caused Marcus Burghardt to crash on the Col d'Iseran during the 2007 Tour de France?

16. Which Australian band reached number 2 in the UK charts in 1971 with 'The Pushbike Song'?

17. Which European capital has hosted the Road World Championships the most times?

18. Which Belgian, who died in 1992, was the first man to win the amateur and professional World Championship Road Race?

19. What prize is awarded to the winner of the Kuurne–Brussels–Kuurne one day race?
    a) a toy bear b) a toy donkey c) a toy lion

20. What is the narrowest overall margin of victory in the Giro d'Italia?
    a) 7 seconds b) 9 seconds c) 11 seconds

Answers to Quiz 73: Vuelta a España

1. Malcolm Elliott
2. Fabio Parra
3. Michael Wright (in 1968)
4. Caja Rural, Cofidis, and Team NetApp-Endura
5. André Greipel
6. Daniel Martin
7. France
8. Malcolm Elliott and Sean Yates
9. Luis Herrera, Oscar Vargas, Juan Martin Farfan, and Felix Cardenas
10. Steve Cummings, Ian Stannard, and Ben Swift
11. True
12. Philip Deignan
13. Sean Kelly and Laurent Jalabert
14. Barry Hoban
15. Rudi Altig, Rolf Wolfshohl, and Jan Ullrich
16. Delio Rodriguez
17. Jan Janssen and Joop Zoetemelk
18. Bauke Mollema
19. Orange
20. 1935

DIFFICULT

Quiz 75: World Road Race Championships part 1

1. Which famous motor-racing circuit hosted the first ever World Road Race Championship?

2. Riders from which country have won the most World Championship Road Races?

3. Who was the first Irishman to make the podium in the World Road Race?

4. Which Dane finished third in 2008 and second in 2010?

5. Who in 1997 became the last Frenchman to win the World Championship Road Race?

6. Which Italian was the first World Road Race Champion?

7. Which British racing circuit was the venue for the 1982 World Road Race?

8. Which Australian port hosted the 2010 Road World Championships?

9. Who had four top-three finishes between 2003 and 2012 without ever winning the rainbow jersey?

10. In 1957, which Belgian became the first post-war rider to win the title in back to back years?

11. Which fellow Belgian repeated that feat in 1960 and 1961?

12. The first Road World Championships hosted in Britain were held in 1970 in which city?

13. Who was runner-up in the Women's World Championship Road Race for five successive years between 2007 and 2011?

14. Which Australian finished in third place in the 2010 World Championship Road Race?

15. Who was the leading British finisher at the 2012 World Championship Road Race?

16. Which sprinter won his only World Championship Road Race at Limburg in 2002?

17. In 2007, who became only the fifth man to defend the title?

18. Which Asian capital is set to host the Road World Championships in 2016?

19. The 2012 World Championship Road Race was contested over what distance?
a) 264km b) 269km c) 274km

20. In which year did the first World Road Race Championship take place?
a) 1922 b) 1927 c) 1932

Answers to Quiz 74: Pot Luck

1. Sir Bradley Wiggins
2. Eight
3. Polish
4. Kirkcaldy
5. Belgian
6. Brad McGee
7. Mark Cavendish
8. Geraint Thomas
9. Martyn Irvine
10. Critérium du Dauphiné
11. London
12. Costa Rica
13. Five
14. Ben Swift
15. A stray dog
16. The Mixtures
17. Copenhagen
18. Jean Aerts
19. A toy donkey
20. 11 seconds

DIFFICULT

Quiz 76: Pot Luck

1. Who was the first British rider to win the Critérium du Dauphiné?

2. Prior to 2012, who were the last two riders from the same country to finish first and second in the Tour de France?

3. Aged just 21 years, 8 months, who in 1979 became the youngest post-war winner of the Giro d'Italia?

4. Which Briton finished second overall in the 2008 Tour of California?

5. Which Dutch province hosted the 2012 World Road Race Championship?

6. Which Spaniard was the only rider to win more than one stage in the 2012 Critérium du Dauphiné?

7. Which Slovak rider made the podium at the 2010 Vuelta a España?

8. BLRC were the initials of which organization that campaigned to promote road racing in Britain?

9. The junior world championships are for cyclists under what age?

10. Which Liverpudlian won the Milk Race in 1986 and the Tour of Britain in 1987?

11. Stefano Garzelli was one of two 39-year-olds to start the 2013 Giro d'Italia. Which German, riding for RadioShack-Leopard, was the other?

12. In which decade were the UCI world rankings introduced?

13. Which Briton won the Men's Scratch race at the 2012 World Track Championships?

14. What colour stripe appears highest on the rainbow jersey?

15. And what colour stripe is lowest on the rainbow jersey?

16. Who was the only Frenchman to make the podium of the World Road Race Championship between 2000 and 2012?

17. What is the name of Andy and Frank Schleck's father, who was also a professional cyclist in the 1960s and 1970s?

18. The first ever British Tour Series race took place in which city?

19. How long was the shortest ever Tour de France road stage?
    a) 26km
    b) 36km
    c) 46km

20. What is Sir Bradley Wiggins' best finish in the Giro d'Italia?
    a) 24th
    b) 40th
    c) 71st

Answers to Quiz 75: World Road Race Championships part 1

1. Nürburgring	11. Rik Van Looy
2. Belgium	12. Leicester
3. Shay Elliott	13. Marianne Vos
4. Matti Breschel	14. Allan Davis
5. Laurent Brochard	15. Jonathan Tiernan-Locke
6. Alfredo Binda	16. Mario Cipollini
7. Goodwood	17. Paolo Bettini
8. Geelong	18. Doha, Qatar
9. Alejandro Valverde	19. 269km
10. Rik Van Steenbergen	20. 1927

DIFFICULT

Quiz 77: Tour de France part 2

1. Who was the first native English-speaker to win the white jersey for the best young rider?

2. Which mountain has featured in the Tour de France more than any other?

3. Who was the first Dutch rider to win the Tour?

4. Who was the last rider to win the Tour de France in their first appearance in the race?

5. What was the first city outside France to host the start of the Tour?

6. Which Rabobank rider was the leading Dutch finisher in the 2012 Tour de France?

7. Who is the only rider to have won five consecutive stages of the Tour de France?

8. Which British-born, Belgian-raised cyclist enjoyed stage victories in 1965, 1967, and 1973?

9. What is the longest gap between a rider winning his first and second Tour de France?

10. Which rider won those two races?

11. Which Polish rider in 1987 became the first East European to wear the leader's yellow jersey?

12. Who are the two riders to have won the stage at Alpe d'Huez who have also won the Tour de France in the same year?

13. Which rider has appeared in the overall top three the most times?

14. The highest ever finish to a Tour stage, some 2,645m, took place in 2011 on top of which Col?

15. Who held on to the yellow jersey for six days of the 1983 Tour despite suffering a broken shoulder?

16. Who holds the record for the fastest time trial of over 40km in Tour de France history?

17. The first ever stage of the Tour de France saw riders race from Paris to which city?

18. In what position did Miguel Indurain finish in his last Tour de France?

19. How long was the first stage of the first Tour?
    a) 267km b) 367km c) 467km

20. Since 1926, how many times has the Tour de France started in Paris?
    a) never b) once c) twice

Answers to Quiz 76: Pot Luck

1. Brian Robinson (in 1961)
2. Bernard Hinault and Laurent Fignon (in 1984)
3. Giuseppe Saronni
4. David Millar
5. Limburg
6. Daniel Moreno
7. Peter Velits
8. British League of Racing Cyclists
9. 19
10. Joey McLoughlin
11. Danilo Honda
12. 1980s
13. Ben Swift
14. Blue
15. Green
16. Anthony Geslin (in 2005)
17. Johny Schleck
18. Milton Keynes
19. 46km
20. 40th

DIFFICULT

Quiz 78: Pot Luck

1. Who was the leading non-European finisher in the 2012 Tour de France?

2. Prior to joining Astana, Vincenzo Nibali was a member of which team?

3. Who was the first Irishman to win a stage in the Giro d'Italia?

4. In which city was British rider Max Sciandri born?

5. Which team won the first season of the British Tour Series?

6. What nationality is Ramūnas Navardauskas?

7. Who was the only Spaniard to win a stage on the 2013 Giro d'Italia?

8. Who are the three riders to have won the Tour de France precisely three times?

9. Which British rider won the first women's Gent–Wevelgem race in 2012?

10. What was the last British city to host the World Cyclo-cross Championships?

11. The first edition of the Tour de France was sponsored by which newspaper?

12. Which Italian, who won the Tour de France green jersey in 1968, once had a heart attack during a race but still carried on to the finish?

13. Which Briton finished fourth in the 2013 Omloop Het Nieuwsblad?

14. A 'gregario' is the Italian name for what?

15. Who was the first rider to be ranked number one in the world using the UCI rankings?

16. Which former Classic winner is the founder of a coffee company called Big Maggy's?

17. The Madonna del Ghisallo climb is a feature of which annual classic?

18. Who was the only member of Team Sky's 2012 Tour de France starters who did not finish the race?

19. The 2013 Giro d'Italia was which edition of the race?
    a) 86th b) 91st c) 96th

20. How much prize money did the winner of the 2012 Tour de France receive?
    a) €400,000 b) €450,000 c) €500,000

Answers to Quiz 77: Tour de France part 2

1. Phil Anderson
2. Col du Tourmalet
3. Jan Janssen
4. Laurent Fignon
5. Amsterdam
6. Laurens ten Dam
7. François Faber
8. Michael Wright
9. Ten years
10. Gino Bartali
11. Lech Piasecki
12. Fausto Coppi and Carlos Sastre
13. Raymond Poulidor (with eight appearances)
14. Col du Galibier
15. Pascal Simon
16. David Millar
17. Lyon
18. 11th
19. 467km
20. Once (in 2003)

DIFFICULT

Quiz 79: Classics

1. Who is the only rider to have won every single-day Classic?

2. Which Swiss rider claimed his maiden Classic win in the 2011 Giro di Lombardia?

3. Sean Kelly won four of the five 'Monuments'. Which one did he fail to win?

4. Who was the first British rider to win Milan–San Remo?

5. The climb of the Kemmelberg is a feature of which one-day Classic?

6. Who holds the record for the most Giro di Lombardia wins with five?

7. Why were Leif Hoste, Peter Van Petegem, and Vladimir Gusev disqualified from the 2006 edition of Paris–Roubaix?

8. Who in 1997 became the first and so far only Dane to win the Tour of Flanders?

9. Which Team Sky rider won Omloop Het Nieuwsblad in 2010?

10. Which multiple winner said, 'A Paris–Roubaix without rain is not a true Paris–Roubaix. Throw in a little snow as well, it's not serious'?

11. Despite its name, Paris–Roubaix doesn't actually start in Paris. In which city does the race start?

12. Which Team Sky rider finished second in La Flèche Wallonne in 2013?

13. Who is the only British rider to have won Gent–Wevelgem?

14. In 1994, which Ukrainian became the first rider from Eastern Europe to win Paris–Roubaix?

Answers – page 165

15. Whose third-place finish in 1987 was the last time a British rider made the podium at Amstel Gold?

16. Which Belgian rider won Paris–Roubaix in 1972, 1974, 1975, and 1977?

17. Kim Andersen was the first Danish winner of La Flèche Wallone. Who in 1998 became the second?

18. Which Briton finished in second place at Gent–Wevelgem in 2007?

19. In which year was the Amstel Gold race held for the first time?
    a) 1956 b) 1961 c) 1966

20. What scuppered Thomas Wegmuller's chances of winning Paris–Roubaix in the closing stages of the the 1988 race?
    a) he was knocked off his bike by a dog
    b) a plastic bag got stuck in his derailleur
    c) he punctured 50m from the finish line

Answers to Quiz 78: Pot Luck

1. Tejay van Garderen
2. Liquigas
3. Shay Elliott
4. Derby
5. Halfords-Bikehut
6. Lithuanian
7. Beñat Intxausti
8. Philippe Thys, Louison Bobet, and Greg LeMond
9. Lizzie Armitstead
10. Leeds
11. L'Auto
12. Franco Bitossi
13. Geraint Thomas
14. A domestique
15. Sean Kelly
16. Magnus Bäckstedt
17. Giro di Lombardia
18. Kanstantsin Siutsou
19. 96th
20. €450,000

DIFFICULT

Quiz 80: Pot Luck

1. Which British rider won the Critérium du Dauphiné in 1990?

2. The first three stages of the 2010 Giro d'Italia were held in which country?

3. The record for the fastest ever individual time trial of over 20km in Tour de France history was set in 1989 by which rider?

4. Excluding Wiggins and Froome, who was the best placed Team Sky finisher at the 2012 Tour de France?

5. Which Argos-Shimano rider was the only German to win a stage of the 2013 Giro d'Italia?

6. Which two riders were on the title winning team in the British Pro Tour in all of the first three seasons of the series?

7. To the nearest minute, what is the largest margin of overall victory in a post-war Tour de France?

8. Who in 1952 recorded that mammoth victory?

9. How many days did Sean Kelly spend in the yellow jersey at the Tour de France?

10. What percentage of stages in the 2013 Giro d'Italia were won by British riders?

11. Who was the first Estonian rider to wear the Tour de France yellow jersey?

12. The first bike path was built in which country?

13. 'Watching the Wheels Go Round' was the title of the 1981 autobiography of which British rider?

14. Which Dutch rider's victories include the 2011 Tour of Oman and the 2012 Tour of California?

15. Which two-time Giro d'Italia winner took part in the 2012 Tour of Britain?

16. Who holds the record for winning the Tour de France at the highest average speed?

17. What colour jersey is worn by the leader of the King of the Mountains competition in the Tour Down Under?

18. Which German started and completed all three Grand Tour races in 2011?

19. What is the largest starting field in the history of the Giro d'Italia?
    a) 289
    b) 298
    c) 308

20. Sir Bradley Wiggins has a tattoo that features the cover of an album by which band?
    a) Oasis
    b) The Smiths
    c) The Prodigy

Answers to Quiz 79: Classics

1. Rik Van Looy
2. Oliver Zaugg
3. Tour of Flanders
4. Tommy Simpson (in 1964)
5. Gent-Wevelgem
6. Fausto Coppi
7. They rode through a railway level crossing
8. Rolf Sørensen
9. Juan Antonio Flecha
10. Sean Kelly
11. Compiègne
12. Sergio Henao
13. Barry Hoban
14. Andrei Tchmil
15. Malcolm Elliott
16. Roger De Vlaeminck
17. Bo Hamburger
18. Roger Hammond
19. 1966
20. A plastic bag got stuck in his derailleur

DIFFICULT

Quiz 81: Sprinters

1. Which Belgian sprinter was disqualified from the 1997 Tour de France after throwing a bottle at rival Frédéric Moncassin?

2. Who won the opening stage of the Tour de France five times between 1956 and 1961?

3. 'The Ogre' was the nickname of which two-time world champion and three-time Tour de France points winner?

4. Which sprinter won five stages during the 2005 Vuelta a España?

5. Who finished runner-up in Milan–San Remo and the Tour of Flanders in 2013?

6. 'Cuore mato' (Mad Heart) was the nickname of which Italian sprinter who won the Tour de France green jersey in 1968?

7. The fastest ever stage in the history of the Tour de France was won in 1999 by which Italian sprinter?

8. How tall is sprinter Tom Boonen?

9. Which Belgian, a member of a famous cycling family, in 1966 became the youngest winner of the Tour de France green jersey?

10. Which sprinter holds the record for the most runner-up stage finishes in the Tour de France?

11. Which French national champion likes to keep in trim in the off-season by boxing?

12. Which Dutchman, the son of a famous sprinter, won the points competition in the 2012 Tour of Britain?

13. In 2010, who became the first Spaniard to win Paris–Tours?

14. Who finished second in the green jersey competition at the 2011 Tour de France despite not winning a single stage?

15. Who won six consecutive stage victories at the Dauphiné Libéré in 1975?

16. Which sprinter was Koen De Kort describing when he said, 'You've got to kill him three times to bring him down'?

17. Which Belgian sprinter, who won the Tour de France green jersey in 1988, was nicknamed 'Die Kleine' (The Small One)?

18. Prior to Peter Sagan, who was the last rider to win the green jersey on his Tour de France debut?

19. How many stages did Mario Cipollini win in his Grand Tour career?
    a) 55 b) 56 c) 57

20. What was the prize money awarded to the winner of the green jersey at the 2013 Tour de France?
    a) €20,000 b) €22,500 c) €25,000

Answers to Quiz 80: Pot Luck

1.	Robert Millar	11.	Jaan Kirsipuu
2.	The Netherlands	12.	USA
3.	Greg LeMond	13.	Barry Hoban
4.	Michael Rogers	14.	Robert Gesink
5.	John Degenkolb	15.	Ivan Basso
6.	Ed Clancy and Andy Tennant	16.	Oscar Pereiro (at 40.788kph in 2006)
7.	28m 17s	17.	White with green spots
8.	Fausto Coppi	18.	Sebastian Lang
9.	One	19.	298
10.	30%	20.	The Prodigy

DIFFICULT

Quiz 82: Pot Luck

1. 'Hunger' was the title of the 2013 autobiography by which successful rider?

2. Which Dane won the Combativity Award at the 2012 Tour de France?

3. Who was Britain's sole representative in the 2012 Men's Road World Championship Time Trial in 2012?

4. Which Spanish climber, who died at the age of 50 in 1996, spent 19 days in the leader's jersey at the Giro but never won the race?

5. 'Lo Sceriffo' (The Sheriff) was the nickname of which former World Champion and four time points winner at the Giro d'Italia?

6. Who in 1993 became the first Latvian rider to win a stage of the Giro d'Italia?

7. Which British rider finished on the podium at the 2013 Tour Down Under?

8. Which Dutchman won Amstel Gold five times between 1977 and 1982?

9. The final round of the 2012 British Tour Series featured a team time trial named after which rider?

10. Which midland city hosted that team time trial?

11. Which British rider finished 167th out of 168 finishers in the 2013 Giro d'Italia?

12. Which former Paris–Roubaix winner was appointed Minister for Sport in Moldova in 2006?

13. Which team won the Team competition at the 2013 Giro d'Italia?

14. The 2013 Giro d'Italia was the first time two Polish riders finished in the top ten of a Grand Tour. Which two riders were they?

15. Who topped the UCI year-end rankings for six consecutive years from 1984 until 1989?

16. Who was the top-ranked rider on the UCI World Tour in 2012?

17. Which Briton won the Women's Keirin and Sprint titles at the 2013 World Track Championships?

18. Harry Watson was the first rider from which country to compete in the Tour de France?

19. Double King of the Mountains points were awarded in how many stages of the 2013 Tour de France?
    a) two b) three c) four

20. How long was the longest solo breakaway that ended with a stage win in the history of the Tour de France?
    a) 233km b) 243km c) 253km

Answers to Quiz 81: Sprinters

1. Tom Steels
2. André Darrigade
3. Freddy Maertens
4. Alessandro Petacchi
5. Peter Sagan
6. Franco Bitossi
7. Mario Cipollini
8. 6ft 4in (1.92m)
9. Willy Planckaert
10. Erik Zabel
11. Nacer Bouhanni
12. Boy Van Poppel
13. Oscar Freire
14. José Joaquin Rojas
15. Freddy Maertens
16. John Degenkolb
17. Eddy Planckaert
18. Olaf Ludwig
19. 57
20. €25,000

DIFFICULT

Quiz 83: Climbers

1. Who was stripped of his stage win at Alpe d'Huez in 1978 after he tried to provide a false urine sample?

2. In 2002, who became the first Mexican to win the Mountains prize at the Giro d'Italia?

3. Who are the two climbers to have won the King of the Mountains in all three Grand Tours?

4. Which two-time Giro d'Italia winner was nicknamed 'Bimbo'?

5. Who was knocked off his bike while climbing Alpe d'Huez in the 1999 Tour de France but still went on to win the stage?

6. Which Colombian won stages of the Critérium du Dauphiné in 2012 and the Volta a Catalunya and Tour of the Basque Country in 2013?

7. With seven wins, who holds the record for the most King of the Mountains victories in the Giro d'Italia?

8. Which overall race winner was the first rider to ever wear the Tour de France polka-dot jersey?

9. Which Spanish climber, who won the King of the Mountains six times, was known as the 'Eagle of Toledo'?

10. 'Clavette' was the nickname of which climber who won the Tour de France King of the Mountains jersey in 1990?

11. Who was André Leducq describing when he said, 'He climbs like artists paint water colours, without any apparent extra effort'?

12. Which Vini Fantini-Selle Italia rider won the Mountains prize at the 2012 Giro d'Italia?

13. Which Tour de France winner won three stages at the Col d'Izoard in the 1950s?

14. Who was the last rider to win the King of the Mountains at the Giro d'Italia more than once (in 2001 and 2003)?

15. Which two Dutch riders won the Tour de France stage at Alpe d'Huez in 1988 and 1989 respectively?

16. In which year was a prize for the Tour de France King of the Mountains awarded for the first time?

17. Who is the only Venezuelan to win the King of the Mountains at the Giro d'Italia?

18. Which rider was sometimes known in the press as 'Monsieur Pi-pi' after an unfortunately timed pit stop at the 1956 Giro d'Italia?

19. In which year was the polka-dot jersey awarded to the leading Tour de France climber for the first time?
a) 1935 b) 1955 c) 1975

20. What was the prize money for winning the King of the Mountains competition at the 2013 Tour de France?
a) €25,000 b) €35,000 c) €45,000

Answers to Quiz 82: Pot Luck

1. Sean Kelly
2. Chris Anker Sørensen
3. Alex Dowsett
4. José Manuel Fuente
5. Francesco Moser
6. Piotr Ugrumov
7. Geraint Thomas
8. Jan Raas
9. Tommy Godwin
10. Stoke-on-Trent
11. Adam Blythe
12. Andrei Tchmil
13. Team Sky
14. Przemyslaw Niemiec and Rafal Majka
15. Sean Kelly
16. Joaquim Rodríguez
17. Becky James
18. New Zealand
19. Three
20. 253km

DIFFICULT

Quiz 84: Pot Luck

1. Which broadcaster wrote the best-selling book 'How I Won the Yellow Jumper: Dispatches from the Tour de France'?

2. 'The Pocket Rocket' was the nickname of which British sprinter?

3. Sir Bradley Wiggins won a bronze medal at the 2004 Olympics in which event?

4. What nationality is Team Sky rider Kanstantsin Sivtsov?

5. Excluding Italians, riders from which country have spent the most days wearing the leader's jersey of the Giro d'Italia?

6. Who said, 'Boil it down, my job is to get our sponsor's logo on that finishing line'?

7. Which French rider is known as 'Le Chou-Chou' (Sweetheart)?

8. Prolific Tweeter Michelle Cound is the girlfriend of which high-profile rider?

9. Which British rider, racing with the BMC team, finished fourth overall at the 2013 Tour of Qatar?

10. Who topped the UCI end-of-year world rankings in 1995, 1996, and 1997 and then again in 1999?

11. Between 1985 and 1989, the Tour de France featured an intermediate sprints competition. What colour jersey was worn by the leader of that contest?

12. Who are the three Italians to have won both the Giro d'Italia and the Vuelta a España?

13. Prior to Geraint Thomas, who was the last Welshman to ride the Tour de France?

14. Which future Tour de France winner won the summit finish at Col d'Aubisque at the 1985 Tour?

15. Which British Olympian made his UK motorsport debut in the Radical SR1 Cup in June 2013?

16. In 2008, which Giro podium finisher also went on to complete the Tour de France and the Vuelta a España?

17. Which team won the team time trial at the 2013 Giro d'Italia?

18. Which Australian won the points title in the 2012 British Tour Series?

19. Why was the climb to Sestriere at the 2013 Giro d'Italia cancelled?
    a) an earthquake
    b) a strike
    c) heavy snow

20. How many riders took part in the 2012 Men's Road World Championship Time Trial?
    a) 48
    b) 58
    c) 68

Answers to Quiz 83: Climbers

1. Michel Pollentier
2. Julio Perez Cuapio
3. Federico Bahamontes and Luis Herrera
4. Ivan Gotti
5. Giuseppe Guerini
6. Nairo Quintana
7. Gino Bartali
8. Joop Zoetemelk
9. Federico Bahamontes
10. Thierry Claveyrolat
11. Fausto Coppi
12. Matteo Rabottini
13. Louison Bobet
14. Fredy González
15. Steven Rooks and Gert-Jan Theunise
16. 1933
17. José Rujano
18. Charly Gaul
19. 1975
20. €25,000

DIFFICULT

Quiz 85: Track World Championships

1. What was the first South American country to host the Track World Championships?

2. The Men's Scratch Race at the 2013 World Championship was raced over what distance?

3. Which country has won the most most gold medals in the history of the Track World Championships?

4. Which A-level student was part of Great Britain's victorious 2013 Women's Team Pursuit line up?

5. Aaron Gate was the only rider from which country to win gold at the 2013 World Championships?

6. What was the only Asian country to win a gold medal at the 2013 World Championships?

7. What was the quartet that in 2005 won Britain's first gold in the Team Pursuit in the professional era of the World Championships?

8. What is the only Asian country to have hosted the Track World Championships?

9. Why were the 2003 World Championships held in Germany rather than in China as was originally planned?

10. In which decade were the Track World Championships held indoors for the first time?

11. Aged just 27, which Olympic gold medallist was the oldest member of Britain's 2013 Track World Championship squad?

12. The Hisense Arena, which hosted a recent Track World Championships, is in which city?

13. When was the last year that Britain failed to win a gold medal at the Track World Championships?

Answers – page 177

14. What was the first British city to host the Track World Championships?

15. Which town in Denmark hosted the Track World Championships in 2002 and 2010?

16. Former Keirin World Champion Keum Mulder represents which country?

17. In a keirin race, the motorbike paces the riders for how many metres?

18. How many gold medals did Britain's men win at the 2009 World Championships?

19. In which year did the first Track World Championships take place?
    a) 1893 b) 1900 c) 1907

20. Which country hosted the inaugural Championships?
    a) France b) Italy c) USA

Answers to Quiz 84: Pot Luck

1. Ned Boulting
2. Steve Joughin
3. Madison
4. Belarussian
5. Belgium
6. Mark Cavendish
7. Thomas Voeckler
8. Chris Froome
9. Adam Blythe
10. Laurent Jalabert
11. Red
12. Vincenzo Nibali, Felice Gimondi, and Giovanni Battaglin
13. Colin Lewis (in 1967)
14. Stephen Roche
15. Sir Chris Hoy
16. Marzio Bruseghin
17. Team Sky
18. Bernard Sulzberger
19. Heavy snow
20. 58

DIFFICULT

Quiz 86: Pot Luck

1. Which British rider was runner-up in the 1988 edition of Gent–Wevelgem?

2. Which three teams were awarded wild-card entries into the 2013 Tour de France?

3. In which year did Cadel Evans make his Grand Tour debut?

4. Which Spaniard is the only man to complete the Giro, Tour, and Vuelta in the same season on four separate occasions?

5. Prior to Jurgen Van Den Broeck in 2010, who was the last Belgian to enjoy a top five finish in the Tour de France?

6. Which Australian Tour veteran was appointed as a performance director at BMC in 2012?

7. David Millar was one of only two British riders to take part in Paris–Nice in 2013. Which Team Sky rider was the other?

8. Who was the last Italian rider to win Milan–San Remo?

9. Which former Norwegian paratrooper rode in the Tour de France, collecting a famous win at Luz-Ardiden in 1987?

10. Which Spanish rider was tragically killed in freak circumstances when a garage door crashed down on him in 2011?

11. Which team was the winner of the 2012 British Tour Series?

12. Which race is mentioned in Ernest Hemingway's novel 'The Sun Also Rises'?

13. The Indira Gandhi Velodrome is in which city?

14. The 12% climb known as the 'Cauberg' is a feature of which Classic?

15. Which Australian was the only rider to win two stages in the 2013 Paris–Nice?

16. Who was the subject of the 2009 biography 'Close to Flying'?

17. In which decade were categories given to Tour de France climbs for the first time?

18. Which Briton won the points competition at Paris–Nice in 2012?

19. Who was the youngest Tour de France winner out of the following riders?
    a) Laurent Fignon
    b) Bernard Hinault
    c) Jan Ullrich

20. What is the smallest ever starting field for the Giro d'Italia?
    a) 54
    b) 64
    c) 74

Answers to Quiz 85: Track World Championships

1. Venezuela
2. 15km
3. France
4. Elinor Barker
5. New Zealand
6. Hong Kong
7. Steve Cummings, Rob Hayles, Paul Manning, and Chris Newton
8. Japan
9. There was an outbreak of the disease SARS
10. 1950s
11. Ed Clancy
12. Melbourne
13. 2001
14. Glasgow
15. Ballerup
16. The Netherlands
17. 1,400m
18. None
19. 1893
20. USA

DIFFICULT

Quiz 87: Books

Which riders were the subject of the following biographies and autobiographies?

1. 'Sex, Lies, and Handelbar Tape'

2. 'Rough Ride'

3. 'In Pursuit of Glory'

4. 'Between the Lines'

5. 'It's Not About the Bike: My Journey Back to Life'

6. 'Boy Racer'

7. 'Flying Scotsman'

8. 'We Were Young and Carefree'

9. 'Racing Through the Dark'.

10. 'Domestique: The Real-life Ups and Downs of a Tour Pro'

11. 'Born to Ride'

12. 'Half Man, Half Bike'

13. 'The Secret Race: Inside the Hidden World of the Tour de France: Doping, Cover-ups, and Winning at All Costs'

14. 'Easy Rider: My Life on a Bike'

15. 'One Way Road'

16. 'Fallen Angel'

17. 'Inside the Peloton: My Life as a Professional Cyclist'

18. 'Put Me Back on My Bike'

19. 'Stages of Light and Dark'

20. 'Sprinter: The Life and Times of a Professional Road Racer'

Answers to Quiz 86: Pot Luck

1. Sean Yates
2. Europcar, Cofidis, and Sojasun
3. 2002 (in the Giro d'Italia)
4. Marino Lejarreta
5. Claude Criquielion
6. Alan Peiper
7. Jonathan Tiernan-Locke
8. Filippo Pozzato
9. Dag-Otto Lauritzen
10. Xavier Tondo
11. Endura Racing
12. Tour of the Basque Country
13. Delhi
14. Amstel Gold
15. Richie Porte
16. Cadel Evans
17. 1940s
18. Sir Bradley Wiggins
19. Laurent Fignon
20. 54

DIFFICULT

Quiz 88: Pot Luck

1. Who in 1996 became the second Russian rider to win the Giro d'Italia?

2. In which year did women first compete in a road race at the Olympic Games?

3. Prior to Sir Chris Hoy in 2008, who was the last British rider to win the World Championship Sprint title?

4. The 2013 Tour de France featured how many mountain-top finishes?

5. Which Kent-born rider, who won the British Road Race Championship in 2009, was brought up in Austin, Texas?

6. Which German started and finished all three Grand Tour races in 2008?

7. With 57 stages in the lead, who has worn the yellow jersey in Paris–Nice the most times?

8. Which Frenchman staged a 243km breakaway to win the stage from Arras to Le Havre in the 1991 Tour de France?

9. La Tropicale Amissa Bongo is a UCI race held in which African country?

10. Which Tour de France King of the Mountains winner won La Tropicale Amissa Bongo in 2009, 2010, and 2011?

11. Which Belgian, two-time Tour de France runner-up and World Road Race Champion, died in a crash during a track race in Antwerp in 1956?

12. Which former Tour de France winner is an ambassador for the Damien Foundation which combats leprosy in the developing world?

13. Who are the three Italians to have won the Tour de France twice?

14. Cadel Evans made his professional road debut riding for which Italian team?

15. Who were the five riders to wear the yellow jersey during the 2011 Tour de France?

16. Who in 1987 was the last Dutch rider to win the Tour de France green jersey?

17. Which alliteratively named rider was the first Norwegian to take part in the Tour de France?

18. 'Fiets' is the word for a bicycle in what language?

19. Swiss rider Tony Rominger was in fact born in which country?
    a) Denmark b) Norway c) Sweden

20. What is the largest margin of victory on a single stage of the Tour de France?
    a) 20m 31s b) 21m 48s c) 22m 50s

Answers to Quiz 87: Books

1.	Jacques Anquetil	11.	Stephen Roche
2.	Paul Kimmage	12.	Eddy Merckx
3.	Bradley Wiggins	13.	Tyler Hamilton
4.	Victoria Pendleton	14.	Rob Hayles
5.	Lance Armstrong	15.	Robbie McEwen
6.	Mark Cavendish	16.	Fausto Coppi
7.	Graeme Obree	17.	Nicolas Roche
8.	Laurent Fignon	18.	Tommy Simpson
9.	David Millar	19.	Bjarne Riis
10.	Charly Wegelius	20.	Malcolm Elliott

DIFFICULT

Quiz 89: The 2012 Olympics

1. Who was the only British rider to win a bronze medal on the track at London 2012?

2. Lee Wai Sze won which country's only cycling medal in the Women's Keirin?

3. What was the name of the course that hosted the Cross-Country Mountain Bike races at London 2012?

4. Which team won bronze in the Men's Team Pursuit?

5. Which Chinese rider won two silvers and a bronze at London 2012 but just missed out on gold?

6. Who was the only New Zealander to win an individual medal on the track at London 2012?

7. Which Latvian won the Men's BMX race?

8. Which British rider crashed in the final of the Men's BMX race?

9. Which member of Britain's 2012 cycling team is a Cambridge graduate who later studied for a PhD in geotechnical engineering?

10. Which German rider claimed silver in the Women's Time Trial?

11. What was the only country to win two medals in the BMX events at London 2012?

12. Who won Denmark's only track cycling gold at the 2012 Games?

13. In which event was he victorious?

14. Which pair both won bronze medals after a dead heat in the third/fourth place Men's Keirin race?

15. How many British riders completed the Men's Cross-Country Mountain Bike race?

16. Who won bronze in both the Women's Road Race and the Women's Individual Time Trial?

17. How many medals did Spain win in the cycling events of the 2012 Games?

18. Which American woman won silver in the Team Pursuit and Omnium?

19. What was the length of the course in the Men's Road Race?
a) 240km b) 250km c) 260km

20. The British team broke the Men's Team Sprint World Record in 2012. What was their record-breaking time?
a) 42.600s b) 42.700s c) 42.800s

Answers to Quiz 88: Pot Luck

1. Pavel Tonkov
2. 1984
3. Reg Harris
4. Four
5. Kristian House
6. Erik Zabel
7. Eddy Merckx
8. Thierry Marie
9. Gabon
10. Anthony Charteau
11. Stan Ockers
12. Eddy Merckx
13. Ottavio Bottecchia, Gino Bartali, and Fausto Coppi
14. Saeco
15. Philippe Gilbert, Thor Hushovd, Thomas Voeckler, Andy Schleck and Cadel Evans
16. Jean-Paul van Poppel
17. Knud Knudsen
18. Dutch
19. Denmark
20. 22m 50s

DIFFICULT

Quiz 90: Pot Luck

1. Excluding Italy, which country has provided the most riders that have taken part in the Giro d'Italia?

2. Which Team Sky rider was runner-up in the 2013 Critérium du Dauphiné?

3. What make of Japanese bike was famously used in the film 'ET – The Extra Terrestrial'?

4. Which team, that included Zak Dempster and Dean Downing, won the 2011 British Tour Series?

5. Who were the two former Vuelta a España winners who started the 2013 Giro d'Italia?

6. Which Dutch rider needed 31 stitches after crashing into a barbed-wire fence after being knocked over by a TV car during the 2011 Tour de France?

7. The first Cyclo-cross World Championships held outside Europe took place in 2013 in which country?

8. The 2013 Tour de France spent how many days in the Pyrenees?

9. Which Spaniard won the 1995 World Road Race Championship despite riding the last couple of kilometres with a flat tyre?

10. Which motor manufacturer is the sponsor of the King of the Mountains competition in the Tour of Britain?

11. Who in 1999 became the last Dutchman to win Paris–Nice?

12. For one year only, the winner of the Points competition at the Tour de France was awarded a jersey that wasn't green. What colour was it?

13. In which decade was that alternative jersey awarded?

14. In 1950, Ferdinand Kubler became the first rider from which country to win the Tour de France?

15. The climb of Mur de Huy is a feature of the course of which one-day Classic?

16. British pro Jeremy Hunt was born in which country?

17. The famous climb of Alpe d'Huez features how many hairpin bends?

18. Which seaside resort features the longest circuit on the British Tour Series?

19. How many international medals did Sir Chris Hoy win during his distinguished career?
    a) 64 b) 74 c) 84

20. How long was the total distance of the shortest ever Tour de France?
    a) 2,428km c) 2,528km c) 2,628km

Answers to Quiz 89: The 2012 Olympics

1. Ed Clancy
2. Hong Kong
3. Hadleigh Farm
4. New Zealand
5. Guo Shuang
6. Simon Van Velthooven
7. Māris Štrombergs
8. Liam Phillips
9. Emma Pooley
10. Judith Arndt
11. Colombia
12. Lasse Norman Hansen
13. Men's Omnium
14. Simon Van Velthooven and Teun Mulder
15. None
16. Olga Zabelinskaya
17. None
18. Sarah Hammer
19. 250km
20. 42.600s

DIFFICULT

Quiz 91: Olympic Cycling

1. At which Olympic Games was track cycling held indoors for the first time?

2. Which Italian won the 2004 Men's Road Race?

3. Which British rider won bronze in the Men's Points Race at the 2008 Games in Beijing?

4. When was the last year that Britain failed to win a medal in track events at the Olympic Games?

5. With a bronze in the Individual Pursuit, who was the only British woman to win a medal at the 2000 Games in Sydney?

6. Which Kiwi did Sir Bradley Wiggins beat in the final of the 2008 Men's Individual Pursuit?

7. Which Briton won the bronze medal in the same competition?

8. In 2000, who became the first man to win medals in the Olympic Road Race and Road Time Trial?

9. Which British quartet won the Team Pursuit gold at the 2008 Games?

10. Which country did the British team beat in the final to secure that gold?

11. In which year was Mountain Biking introduced to the Olympic programme?

12. Which American finished in fourth place in both the Men's Road Race and Time Trial at the 2012 Games?

13. Which French woman has appeared in more Olympic Games than any other rider?

14. Which Australian did Sir Bradley Wiggins beat in the final of the Individual Pursuit in Athens in 2004?

Answers – page 189

15. In which year did women make their debut in Olympic track events?

16. Which Italian was the first rider to win both an Olympic gold medal and a Grand Tour race?

17. Which Dutch rider holds the record as the woman with the most Olympic cycling medals with six?

18. Which Swiss rider won the Men's Road Race in 1996?

19. Which country has won the most medals in the history of Olympic cycling competition?
a) Australia b) France c) Great Britain

20. In total, the 2012 Olympic Games featured how many cycling events?
a) 16 b) 18 c) 20

Answers to Quiz 90: Pot Luck

1. Spain
2. Richie Porte
3. Kuwahara
4. Rapha Condor-Sharp
5. Juan José Cobo and Vincenzo Nibali
6. Johnny Hoogerland
7. USA
8. Two
9. Abraham Olano
10. Skoda
11. Michael Boogerd
12. Red
13. 1960s
14. Switzerland
15. La Flèche Wallone
16. Canada
17. 21
18. Torquay
19. 84
20. 2,428km

DIFFICULT

Quiz 92: Pot Luck

1. Up to the 2013 race, two British riders had won more than one stage of the Giro d'Italia. Mark Cavendish is one, who is the other?

2. Who was the first British woman to win the world time trial title?

3. Sir Chris Hoy was first inspired to start riding a bike as a six-year-old after watching which film?

4. Which name is shared by a French three-time Olympic gold medallist and a type of Californian sparkling wine?

5. Which Euskaltel-Euskadi rider in 2013 became the first Greek to take part in the Giro d'Italia?

6. Which alliteratively named German won Paris–Nice in 2004, leading the race from start to finish?

7. Three Dutchmen have won two Tour de France stages that finished on Alpe d'Huez. Joop Zoetemelk and Hennie Kuiper were two of them. Who was the third?

8. In which year were professionals allowed to compete in Olympic cycling events for the first time?

9. Who in 2012 became the first British rider to win the Kuurne–Brussels–Kuurne one-day race?

10. Who is the only Danish rider to have won stages in the Tour de France, Giro d'Italia, and Vuelta a España?

11. Which former motor-racing driver, who has taken part in the Le Mans 24 Hour race, appeared in the 2013 British Tour Series?

12. The 2013 Vuelta a España featured how many summit finishes?

13. Which German won the first two editions of the Tour of Beijing in 2011 and 2012?

14. Which Team Sky rider finished on the podium in the 2012 edition of the above race?

Answers – page 191

15. What colour jersey is worn by the leader of the points competition in the Tour of Switzerland?

16. Who were the four former Giro d'Italia winners who started the 2013 race?

17. Which Swiss rider was the last man to win the Giro d'Italia whose first name and surname start with the same letter?

18. Which climber said of doping in the Tour de France, 'When I saw riders with fat asses climbing cols like aeroplanes, I understood what was happening'?

19. The Great Britain women set a world record in the Team Pursuit at the London Olympics. What was their record-breaking time?
    a) 3:15.669 b) 3:16.669 c) 3:17.669

20. What was the distance of the shortest ever Tour de France prologue?
    a) 1km b) 1.2km c) 1.4km

Answers to Quiz 91: Olympic Cycling

1. Montreal in 1976
2. Paolo Bettini
3. Chris Newton
4. 1996
5. Yvonne McGregor
6. Hayden Roulston
7. Steven Burke
8. Jan Ullrich
9. Ed Clancy, Paul Manning, Geraint Thomas and Sir Bradley Wiggins
10. Denmark
11. 1996
12. Taylor Phinney
13. Jeannie Longo
14. Brad McGee
15. 1988
16. Ercole Baldini
17. Leontien van Moorsel
18. Pascal Richard
19. France
20. 18

DIFFICULT

Quiz 93: Tour de France part 3

1. In the Tour de France, what role is carried out by 'un ardoisier'?

2. Who was the last rider to win the green jersey at the Tour de France whose first name and surname start with the same letter?

3. In which decade did the Tour visit Mont Ventoux for the first time?

4. What was the first German city to host the start of the Tour de France?

5. What is the name of the unofficial prize awarded by journalists to the most uncooperative rider on the Tour?

6. True or false – a stage in the 1920 race took the winner over 15 hours to complete?

7. Only once has the Tour de France been won in consecutive years by two different riders sharing the same surname. What was the surname?

8. Who was the leading Spanish finisher in the 2012 Tour de France?

9. In 1930, which member of a famous cycling family won eight stages and finished second in seven others but still failed to win the overall race?

10. Who broke his cheekbone and his jaw on the 16th stage of the 1975 race but still went on to complete it and make the podium?

11. In 1947 Jean Robic became the first rider to do what?

12. Which feature of the Tour de France was won for the first time in 1934 by Frenchman Antonin Magne?

13. Why was Jacky Durand disqualified from the 2002 Tour?

14. True or false – neither Eddy Merckx nor Jacques Anquetil won a Tour stage at Alpe d'Huez?

15. Max Bulla was the first rider from which country to wear the Tour de France yellow jersey?

16. How many stages of the Tour de France did Miguel Indurain win?

17. How old was the oldest man to complete the Tour de France?

18. In which year did an American team appear in the Tour de France for the first time?

19. Why were several riders expelled from the 1906 Tour?
    a) they deliberately punctured a rival's tyre
    b) they took a short cut
    c) they took a train rather than ride up a climb

20. Tour winner Bernard Thévenet grew up in a village called Le Guidon. What does Le Guidon mean in English?
    a) The Handlebar
    b) The Pedal
    c) The Spoke

Answers to Quiz 92: Pot Luck

1. Max Sciandri
2. Emma Pooley
3. ET – The Extra-Terrestrial
4. Paul Masson
5. Ioannis Tamouridis
6. Jörg Jaksche
7. Peter Winnen
8. 1996
9. Mark Cavendish
10. Jesper Skibby
11. Greg Mansell
12. 11
13. Tony Martin
14. Edvald Boasson Hagen
15. White with red polka dots
16. Ryder Hesjedal, Michele Scarponi, Danilo Di Luca, Stefano Garzelli
17. Carlo Clerici
18. Luis Herrera
19. 3:15.669
20. 1km

DIFFICULT

Quiz 94: Pot Luck

1. Who was the first British rider to win a stage of the Giro d'Italia?

2. In which year did BMX events make their debut at the Olympics as medal events?

3. The black, green, and pink jersey is awarded to the best young rider in which stage race?

4. The climb of the Col d'Eze is a feature of which annual stage race?

5. Which legendary film director raised the flag to start the 1950 Tour de France?

6. Many of cycling's biggest races are organized by ASO. For what do the initials ASO stand?

7. Which former Paris–Roubaix winner led the MG Maxifuel team in the 2013 Tour Series?

8. Oude Kwaremont is a climb that features in which one-day 'Monument'?

9. Which two British riders finished on the podium at the 2011 Tour of Beijing?

10. Which Briton finished fourth in the same race?

11. Which male British Olympic gold medallist won a silver medal as a junior in the coxless pairs at the British Rowing Championships?

12. Who was the last rider to win the points competition at the Giro d'Italia whose first name and surname start with the same letter?

13. Who is the only Irish rider to have won stages in all three Grand Tours?

14. Which Spaniard joined the elite group of riders to have won stages in all three Grand Tours after winning on stage 17 of the 2012 Giro?

Answers – page 195

15. Who was the last rider to win the Tour de France while riding for a national rather than a trade team?

16. Which Swiss dandy, who kept a comb in the pocket of his yellow jersey, was nicknamed 'The Pedaller of Charm'?

17. In 2012, Robert Kiserlovski became only the second rider from which country to take part in the Tour de France?

18. Prior to 1992, in which year did a British rider last win Olympic cycling gold?

19. What was the surname of the four Swedish brothers who were world team trial champions from 1967 to 1969?
a) Eriksson b) Lundberg c) Petterson

20. How long was the longest stage in the history of the Tour de France?
a) 462km b) 472km c) 482km

Answers to Quiz 93: Tour de France part 3

1. He sits on a motorbike and writes the time differences between breakaways and the bunch.
2. Jan Janssen
3. 1950s
4. Cologne
5. Le prix citron
6. True
7. Maes (Romain and Sylvère)
8. Haimar Zubeldia
9. Charles Pélissier
10. Eddy Merckx
11. Win the Tour on the last day without having worn the yellow jersey during any of the previous stages
12. Individual time trial
13. He took a tow from a car during a mountain stage.
14. True
15. Austria
16. 12
17. 50
18. 1986
19. The took a train rather than ride up a climb.
20. The Handlebar

DIFFICULT

Quiz 95: World Road Race Championships part 2

1. Which reigning World Champion was killed after being hit by a car in a race in 1971?

2. Who was the last rider to win the World Road Race Championship whose first name and surname start with the same letter?

3. In 2000, who became the first Eastern European rider to win the World Road Race?

4. Who is the only Junior Road Race world champion to have gone on to win the rainbow jersey in the senior race?

5. Who was the last Dutchman to win gold in the Road World Championship?

6. Which team won the Team Time Trial at the 2012 World Road Race Championships?

7. Who is the only Canadian to have made the podium in the Road World Championship?

8. Which German won the Road World Championship Time Trial in 2008?

9. Which winner of the 1999 Junior Road Race won a silver medal in the senior World Championship Road Race in 2008?

10. Which British rider came third in the 2011 Men's Under-23 World Road Race?

11. Who was the last man to win the World Road Race Championship whose surname starts and ends with the same letter?

12. Which Briton won the Women's World Road Race Championship in 1982?

13. Who was the last Swiss rider to win the Men's Road Race?

14. Who is the only Colombian to have won the World Road Race Championship Time Trial?

15. Who is the only gold medallist in the Men's Under-23 Road Race to have gone on to win a Grand Tour?

16. Which German won the Women's Time Trial in both 2011 and 2012?

17. Which Ukrainian won the World Road Race Championship Time Trial in 2000?

18. Who was the last Italian to win the World Road Race Championship?

19. What was the first non-European city to host the Road World Championships?
    a) Brisbane b) Montreal c) Tokyo

20. How many British men have made the podium in the World Championship Road Race?
    a) two b) three c) four

Answers to Quiz 94: Pot Luck

1. Vin Denson
2. 2008
3. Tour Down Under
4. Paris–Nice
5. Orson Welles
6. Amaury Sport Organisation
7. Magnus Bäckstedt
8. Tour of Flanders
9. Chris Froome and David Millar
10. Steve Cummings
11. Sir Chris Hoy
12. Danilo Di Luca
13. Shay Elliott
14. Joaquim Rodríguez
15. Jan Janssen
16. Hugo Koblet
17. Croatia
18. 1920
19. Petterson
20. 482km

DIFFICULT

Quiz 96: Pot Luck

1. Which Irishman claimed his only Giro d'Italia stage win at Sauze d'Oulx in 1986?

2. The phrase 'shut up legs' is most commonly associated with which veteran rider?

3. Which Tour de France winner finished runner-up in Paris–Nice 1984, 1985, 1989, and 1990?

4. In 1989 who became the first (and so far only) British winner of the Tour of Belgium?

5. Who are the three riders (two Aussies and a German) to have won the Tour Down Under more than once?

6. Harry Ryan and Thomas Lance won Olympic gold for Great Britain in which event?

7. Who was the last rider to win the points competition at the Giro d'Italia whose surname starts and ends with the same letter?

8. Which spread-betting firm sponsored the sprints competition in the 2013 British Tour Series?

9. Which Belgian world champion was killed in a car crash en route to the finish of the Tour of Flanders in 1998, aged just 36?

10. How old was the youngest man to complete the Tour de France?

11. Which Team Katusha climber finished third in the 2013 Critérium du Dauphiné?

12. Chris Froome has suffered from which tropical disease?

13. Which Vacansoleil rider suffered a ruptured kidney and spleen, bruised lungs, and three broken ribs after a horrific crash on stage 6 of the 2012 Tour de France?

Answers – page 199

14. Which Danish rider was famously knocked off his bike by the race director in the 1988 Tour of Flanders?

15. Who has finished runner-up in the Tour de France green jersey competition a record four times?

16. In what position did Chris Froome finish on his Tour de France debut?

17. Eddy Merckx made his professional debut riding for which team?

18. Paul Egli was the first rider from which country to wear the yellow jersey at the Tour de France?

19. How long was the course for the Women's Road Race at the London 2012 Olympics?
a) 140.3km b) 145.3km c) 150.3km

20. Riders representing how many different countries started the 2012 Tour de France?
a) 21 b) 31 c) 41

Answers to Quiz 95: World Road Race Championships part 2

1. Jean-Pierre Monseré
2. Luc Leblanc
3. Romāns Vainšteins
4. Greg LeMond
5. Joop Zoetemelk
6. Omega Pharma-Quick Step
7. Steve Bauer
8. Bert Grabsch
9. Damiano Cunego
10. Andrew Fenn
11. Igor Astarloa
12. Mandy Jones
13. Oscar Camenzind
14. Santiago Botero
15. Ivan Basso
16. Judith Arndt
17. Serhiy Honchar
18. Alessandro Ballan
19. Montreal
20. Two

DIFFICULT

Quiz 97: UCI World Tour

1. Which two Canadian cities were on the schedule to host World Tour races in 2013?

2. The 2013 Eneco Tour featured stages in which two countries?

3. What was the top-ranked nation according to the 2012 UCI World Rankings?

4. What was the first UCI World Tour event to take place outside Europe?

5. How many UCI World Tour events did Sir Bradley Wiggins win in 2012?

6. What is the only UCI World Tour event that takes place in Eastern Europe?

7. Who were the two Scandinavians to win UCI World Tour races in 2012?

8. How many of Team Sky's eight starters in the 2010 Giro di Lombardia finished the race?

9. Who was the only Frenchman to win a 2012 UCI World Tour race after triumphing in the Vattenfall Cyclassics?

10. Cadel Evans and Matt Goss were two of the three Aussies to win UCI World Tour events in 2011. Who was the third?

11. Which winner of one of the 2013 Spring Classics failed to earn any ranking points as he rides for a team, MTN Qhubeka, that isn't a World Tour Team?

12. In Grand Tour races, the top how many finishers receive ranking points?

13. How many finishers receive ranking points in the other UCI World Tour events?

Answers – page 201

14. How many ranking points are awarded for winning one of the 'Monuments'?

15. Two Americans won UCI World Tour events in 2010. Tyler Farrar was one. Who was the other, winning the Tour of the Basque Country?

16. Which Aussie won a hat-trick of UCI World Tour events in 2012?

17. Who was the only Kazakh rider to win a UCI World Tour event in 2012?

18. In which one-day classic was he triumphant?

19. How many UCI World Tour ranking points are awarded for winning the Tour de France?
a) 180 b) 190 c) 200

20. The 2013 UCI World Tour comprised how many races?
a) 28 b) 29 c) 30

Answers to Quiz 96: Pot Luck

1. Martin Earley
2. Jens Voigt
3. Stephen Roche
4. Sean Yates
5. Stuart O'Grady, Simon Gerrans, and André Greipel
6. Tandem sprint
7. Tony Rominger
8. IG
9. Rudy Dhaenens
10. 17
11. Daniel Moreno
12. Schistosomiasis (bilharzia)
13. Wout Poels
14. Jesper Skibby
15. Stuart O'Grady
16. 84th
17. Solo-Superia
18. Switzerland
19. 140.3km
20. 31

DIFFICULT

Quiz 98: Pot Luck

1. Which British Member of Parliament is known as 'The Bicycling Baronet'?

2. Who in 2013 became the first Chinese rider to compete in the Giro d'Italia?

3. Which Omega Pharma-Quick Step rider won back-to-back Tour of Belgium titles in 2012 and 2013?

4. Which former French and World Champion was seriously injured after being hit by a car while riding his bike near Montauban in March 2013?

5. The mother of which Olympic champion was made MBE for her services to health care in the UK in 2009, the same year that her son also received an award?

6. Which cycling commentator has an interest in a gold mine in Uganda?

7. Who finished third in Paris–Nice in 2011?

8. What nationality is Team Garmin-Sharp rider Rohan Dennis?

9. Which Dutch rider won the 2013 Tour Down Under?

10. Which rider forgot to take out his cotton-wool nose plugs before the start of the opening prologue of the 2012 Tour de France?

11. Which big name was runner-up in the Tour of Oman and third in Tirreno–Adriatico in 2013?

12. What is the name of Philippe Gilbert's younger brother who rides for the Belgian Accent-Wanty team?

13. Which two East Anglian towns held a British Tour Series event for the first time in 2013?

14. Which alliteratively named Frenchman broke his back after a horrific fall during a descent of the Col de Perjurat in 1960?

15. Which award-winning French film director made the 1962 documentary 'Vive le Tour'?

16. Which Dutch writer wrote the acclaimed cycling novel 'The Rider'?

17. Prior to Mark Cavendish, who was the last British rider to finish in the top three in the Tour de France points competition?

18. Who was the last winner of the Tour de l'Avenir to win the Tour de France?

19. How much prize money was awarded to the winner of the 2013 Giro d'Italia?
a) €80,000 b) €90,000 c) €100,000

20. At its steepest, how steep in degrees was the Olympic Velodrome at London 2012?
a) 40 degrees b) 42 degrees c) 44 degrees

Answers to Quiz 97: UCI World Tour

1. Montreal and Quebec
2. Belgium and the Netherlands
3. Spain
4. Tour Down Under
5. Four
6. Tour of Poland
7. Edvald Boasson Hagen and Lars Petter Nordhaug
8. One
9. Arnaud Démare
10. Cameron Meyer
11. Gerald Ciolek
12. 20
13. 10
14. 100
15. Chris Horner
16. Simon Gerrans
17. Maxim Iglinsky
18. Liège–Bastogne–Liège
19. 200
20. 29

DIFFICULT

Quiz 99: Anagrams

Rearrange the letters to make the name of a well-known cyclist.

1. Roast carbuncle

2. Hires compliance

3. Orange burrito

4. Albino zinc vein

5. Grab reconvened junk

6. Jeered any vagrant

7. Loved a lavender jar

8. Nightmare oats

9. Snorers enhance risk

10. A vagabond lends shoe

11. Lunches amazes

12. Nude maniac goo

13. A cannibal car flea

14. A ship dots clearance

15. Jaded her slyer

16. Lay new tankards

17. Ripple hip giblet

18. Colon cashier

19. Irons manager

20. Canine loofah jaunt

Answers to Quiz 98: Pot Luck

1. Sir George Young
2. Cheng Ji
3. Tony Martin
4. Laurent Jalabert
5. Sir Chris Hoy
6. Paul Sherwen
7. Sir Bradley Wiggins
8. Australian
9. Tom-Jelte Slagter
10. Chris Froome
11. Alberto Contador
12. Jerome
13. Aylsham and Ipswich
14. Roger Rivière
15. Louis Malle
16. Tim Krabbé
17. Max Sciandri
18. Laurent Fignon
19. €90,000
20. 42 degrees

DIFFICULT

Quiz 100: Pot Luck

1. Stoke-on-Trent is one of two places to have hosted a leg of the British Tour Series every year since the competition started. What southern town is the other?

2. Which former winner of the Giro d'Italia, riding for the Vini Fantini-Selle Italia team, was the oldest rider in the 2013 race?

3. Which Australian won the Tour Down Under in 2002 despite being hit by a motorbike during one of the stages?

4. Who was the last Frenchman to win Paris–Nice?

5. Which member of a famous acting family said, 'My father is the Hollywood equivalent of a clean, fillet-brazed frame. My brother is like one of those fat-tubed aluminum Cannondales. I'm more like one of those Taiwanese Masis'?

6. Who were the two Frenchmen to win the Tour de France in the 1970s?

7. Which Belgian won Paris–Roubaix in 1990 after surviving a massive 222km breakaway?

8. Which nephew of a former world champion won the 2012 Tour of Poland?

9. In 2002, who became the first and so far only British winner of the GP Ouest-France?

10. Which cycling broadcaster is the son of a Scottish football international?

11. There is a memorial to which rider, who commited suicide in 1994, on the Col de Mente?

12. After retiring in 1947, which Australian went into politics and later became his country's minister of transport?

13. 'Pinpin' was the nickname of which popular French rider who enjoyed top-ten Tour de France finishes in 1986 and 1988?

14. Who was the first Scottish rider to complete the Tour de France?

15. Which energy snack was the official sponsor of stage winners at the 2012 Tour de France?

16. In the Tour de France, how many green jersey points are awarded to the first man home on a high mountain stage?

17. Which famous British department store briefly sponsored a professional cycling team in the 1990s?

18. How many times did Fausto Coppi win the Vuelta a España?

19. What is the slowest average speed of a winning rider in the Tour de France?
    a) 14.9mph b) 15.9mph c) 16.9mph

20. Why was the prologue of the 1983 Giro d'Italia cancelled?
    a) vandals had damaged the circuit
    b) a strike by protesting metalworkers
    c) unseasonal heavy snow

Answers to Quiz 99: Anagrams

1. Carlos Betancur
2. Michele Scarponi
3. Rigoberto Urán
4. Vincenzo Nibali
5. Jurgen Van Den Broeck
6. Tejay van Garderen
7. Alejandro Valverde
8. Geraint Thomas
9. Chris Anker Sørensen
10. Edvald Boasson Hagen
11. Samuel Sanchez
12. Damiano Cunego
13. Fabian Cancellara
14. Alessandro Petacchi
15. Ryder Hesjedal
16. Andrew Talansky
17. Philippe Gilbert
18. Nicolas Roche
19. Simon Gerrans
20. Juan Antonio Flecha

DIFFICULT

Keeping Score

Keeping Score

Keeping Score

Keeping Score

Keeping Score

Keeping Score

Keeping Score

Keeping Score

Keeping Score

Keeping Score

Get quizzical with the full
Collins quiz range

Available in paperback
and ebook.

Available in paperback
and ebook.

Available in paperback.

Available in paperback
and ebook.

Available in paperback
and ebook.

Available in paperback
and ebook.

Available in paperback
and ebook.

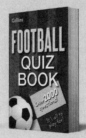

Available in paperback
and ebook.

All **Collins** quiz range titles in paperback are RRP £6.99. Ebook prices may vary.

Find more information on our products at www.collinslanguage.com.
Available to buy from all good booksellers.

Follow us on Twitter @collinsdict   Find Collins Dictionary on Facebook